STATE OF WAR

Political Violence and
Counterinsurgency in Colombia

Human Rights Watch/Americas
(formerly Americas Watch)

Human Rights Watch
New York ◆ Washington ◆ Los Angeles ◆ London

Human Rights Watch/Americas
Human Rights Watch/Americas, fomerly Americas Watch, was established
in 1981 to monitor and promote observance of internationally recognized
human rights in Latin America and the Caribbean. Peter D. Bell is chair;
Stephen L. Kass and Marina Pinto Kaufman are vice chairs; Juan E.
Méndez is the executive director; Cynthia Arnson and Anne Manuel are
associate directors; Robin Kirk is the Andean researcher; MaryJane
Camejo,and Gretta Tovar Siebentritt are research associates; Vanessa
Jiménez and Ben Penglase are associates.

HUMAN RIGHTS WATCH

Human Rights Watch conducts regular, systematic investigations of human rights abuses in some seventy countries around the world. It addresses the human rights practices of governments of all political stripes, of all geopolitical alignments, and of all ethnic and religious persuasions. In internal wars it documents violations by both governments and rebel groups. Human Rights Watch defends freedom of thought and expression, due process and equal protection of the law; it documents and denounces murders, disappearances, torture, arbitrary imprisonment, exile, censorship and other abuses of internationally recognized human rights.

Human Rights Watch began in 1978 with the founding of its Helsinki division. Today, it includes five divisions covering Africa, the Americas, Asia, the Middle East, as well as the signatories of the Helsinki accords. It also includes four collaborative projects on Arms, Free Expression, Prisoners' Rights, and Womens Rights. It now maintains offices in New York, Washington, Los Angeles, London, Moscow, Belgrade, Zagreb and Hong Kong. Human Rights Watch is an independent, nongovernmental organization, supported by contributions from private individuals and foundations. It accepts no government funds, directly or indirectly.

Addresses for Human Rights Watch

485 Fifth Avenue
New York, NY 10017-6104
Tel: (212) 972-8400
Fax: (212) 972-0905
email: hrwatchnyc@igc.apc.org

1522 K Street, N.W., #910
Washington, DC 20005
Tel: (202) 371-6592
Fax: (202) 371-0124
email: hrwatchdc@igc.apc.org

10951 West Pico Blvd., #203
Los Angeles, CA 90064
Tel: (310) 475-3070
Fax: (310) 475-5613
email: hrwatchla@igc.apc.org

90 Borough High Street
London, UK SE1 1LL
Tel: (071) 378-8008
Fax: (071) 378-8029
email: hrwatchuk@gn.org

COLOMBIA, A DREAM OF PEACE

So that in the fields

the barking of dogs

at any dawn

not be the sinister prowl

of wandering death,

let it be a hand clasp,

let it be the warm smile

of an arriving friend

and not the dark jaws

of a threatening rifle.

So that soldiers and guerrillas

not be for each other

grim death sniffing out

tremulous life.

Let bombs of bread and toys explode

and our children run among the debris of kisses.

Lancita... dear soldier...

remember that Jacinto, son of that old peasant,

joined the guerrillas

searching for dawns,

the birth of new days.

Let him not return dead,

don't quench his flame.

Because the old woman waits

clutching her rosary

begging the spirits

to let nothing harm him.

Dear friend... comrade...

Do you remember Chuchito,

the one who played cops and robbers

with you and the other neighborhood boys?

Today, he's a grown man

full of hope,

he joined the army carrying a flag,

symbol of our nation.

Don't cut short his path

setting ambushes

because you yourself must then

carry the news that will part the soul

of that poor mother

who lives next door.

Hunger also

beats the war drum

spawning weapons.

Each rifle takes (in price alone)

a year of food

from a family or house

and serves up breakfasts of hatred and bullets.

Peace, they have dressed you in black

although you are white, white;

or in the blue of shipwrecks

or the sinister red

of spilled blood.

You are neither the green hurricane of the

mountains.

Let all the politicians today cover their faces

and every untouched bride remove her gown

to array you in the white dress of a white cloud.

-Tirso Vélez, Mayor of Tibú, Norte de Santander "Un alcalde en Apuros," *Cien Días,* Vol. 6, No. 22, April-June, 1993, p. 27. Translation by Americas Watch. Following the publication of this poem, Tirso Vélez was charged with terrorism and imprisoned.

CONTENTS

Acknowledgments vii

Introduction viii

PART I

A Panorama of Violence 3

The Declaration of the State of Internal Commotion 6

From State of Emergency to Total War 11

Impunity 16
    Urabá 20
    Trujillo 22
    El Nilo 23
    Los Uvos 25
    Fusagasugá 26
    UNASE 27
    Senior Military Involvement with Paramilitary Group 28

The Report of the *Procuraduría* 29

Irregular Use of the "Public Order" Courts 35

The Erosion of Constitutional Guarantees 40

The Law to Regulate States of Exception 43

Tutela 46

Attacks on Human Rights Monitors 48

The Drug War 51

PART II

The Mobile Brigades 65
    A Pattern of Violations 69
    Mobile Brigade 2 and The Middle Magdalena 73

A Case Study: Meta 84
    Climate of Violence 97
    Impunity 106

Guerrilla Abuses in Conflict Zones 113
    The FARC 118
    The ELN 121
    The EPL 125

PART III

United States Policy 130

Appendix I 140

Appendix II 146

ACKNOWLEDGMENTS

This report was written by Cynthia Arnson, Associate Director of Americas Watch, and Robin Kirk, Andean Researcher for Americas Watch. It was edited by Americas Watch Executive Director Juan E. Méndez. The Report is based on three fact-finding trips to Colombia: in June and October 1992 by Kirk, and in February-March 1993 by Arnson and Kirk. Additional research and editorial assistance was provided by Stephen Goose, Washington Director of the Arms Project; Allyson Collins, Human Rights Watch Research Associate; Vanessa Jiménez, Americas Watch Associate; and Stephen Crandall, Americas Watch intern.

We would like to extend a special and heartfelt thanks to the individuals and groups that helped us gather information and review our findings. They include Reinaldo Botero, Gustavo Gallón, and other members of the *Comisión Andina de Juristas-Seccional Colombiana*; Diego Pérez and the Human Rights team at the *Centro de Investigación y Educación Popular*; the *Colectivo de Abogados "José Alvear Restrepo;"* Father Javier Giraldo and Juan Carlos Gutiérrez of the *Comisión Intercongregacional de Justicia y Paz*; the *Comité Cívico del Meta*; the *Instituto Latinoamericano de Servicios Legales Alternativos*; the *Comité Regional para la Defensa de los Derechos Humanos*; Carlos Vicente de Roux, Presidential Counselor for Human Rights; Jorge Orlando Melo, former Presidential Counselor for Human Rights; the office of the *Defensor del Pueblo*; and Hernando Valencia and the *Oficina de Investigaciones Especiales* of the *Procuraduría General de la Nación*.

Finally, we wish to thank all the Colombians who spoke with us on condition of anonymity. Their names are marked in this text with an asterisk (*).

INTRODUCTION

On November 8, 1992, Colombian President César Gaviria Trujillo declared a "state of internal commotion," invoking provisions of the Colombian Constitution empowering him to adopt emergency measures in the event of "serious disruption of the public order imminently threatening institutional stability, the security of the state, or the peaceful coexistence of the citizenry."[1] A series of emergency decrees restricted civil liberties, granted additional powers to the military, and punished contact or dialogue with insurgent groups. The decrees marked a reversion to authoritarian patterns of rule supposedly left behind with the passage of the 1991 Constitution.[2]

Despite the adoption of emergency measures, however, the government has failed to achieve its central goal: winning a decisive upper hand in the war against Colombia's approximately 7,000 guerrilla insurgents. Indeed, in a military build-up that began even as successful peace talks with the guerrillas were taking place, the Colombian government has devoted ever more resources to war since 1990. A centerpiece of army strategy has been the creation of three Mobile Brigades, elite units of professional soldiers that receive special training and operate in areas of greatest insurgent activity.

Although the government claims that Mobile Brigade soldiers commit fewer human rights abuses than regular troops, information gathered by Americas Watch in this report paints a strikingly different picture. The units have been implicated in a shocking number of abuses, including

---

[1] Article 213, *Constitución Política de Colombia* (Bogotá: Presidencia de la República, 1991), p. 81.

[2] As described below, several of the emergency decrees were ruled unconstitutional by Colombia's Constitutional Court, which automatically reviews the legality of rulings issued during a state of exception. Others, however, have been or are in the process of being converted into permanent legislation. President Gaviria renewed the state of internal commotion twice in 1993, the legal limit established in the Constitution. The state of internal commotion expired in August 1993, although emergency decrees remained in effect through early November.

extra-judicial executions, "disappearances," rapes, torture, the wanton burning of houses, crops, and food, indiscriminate bombings and aerial strafing, beatings, and death threats. These newly-created units not only reinforce existing patterns of abuse -- including the continued formation and fortification of paramilitary groups -- but are pioneering a grisly new attack on Colombia's rural families, particularly those living in isolated areas and most vulnerable to injustice.

Guerrillas of the Simón Bolívar Guerrilla Coordinating Committee (CGSB) have also engaged in a disturbing pattern of violations of international humanitarian law, evidenced by the killing and torture of captured security force officers, selective assassinations of critics, attacks on civilian targets, and the destruction of the environment by repeated bombings of oil pipelines, putting the civilian population in grave danger. In September 1993, the guerrillas launched a new offensive they called "Black September," killing some thirty soldiers and police in the space of two weeks alone.[3] In opening their campaign, the guerrillas ambushed thirteen policemen and the civilian director of Bogotá's water authority near Usme, Cundinamarca. The policemen were killed after being disarmed, a grave violation of international humanitarian law.[4]

The determination of the guerrillas to demonstrate their strength, together with the Colombian government's equal determination to contain and erode the insurgents' fighting capacity, will most probably only prolong the stalemate that has characterized Colombia's thirty-year guerrilla war. But the upswing in fighting, and military strategies of both sides that refuse to respect the neutrality of the civilian population, have sharpened the suffering of Colombian civilians. As one international relief worker told Americas Watch, "when there is more war, the principal

---

[3] Mary Speck, "Colombian guerrillas resume attacks," *Miami Herald*, September 11, 1993.

[4] Gustavo Gallón Giraldo, Letter to *El Tiempo*, September 16, 1993; Reuters, "Colombian Rebels Kill 13 Police in Ambush, *Washington Times*, August 29, 1993.
Common Article 3 of the Geneva Conventions of 1949 prohibits the execution of combatants once they have been placed *hors de combat* by virtue of capture or injury.

victim is the civilian population. They have to collaborate with the guerrillas or with the army. They don't have a choice."[5]

The guerrilla war represents only one, albeit an important, aspect of political violence in Colombia. Yet we have focused this report on the government's counterinsurgency strategy and the guerrillas' equally violative response for several reasons: 1) to highlight the human tragedy of Latin America's longest-running and yet largely forgotten war, 2) to document the growing human rights abuses and violations of international humanitarian law inherent in the strategies of both sides, and 3) to show how the pattern of rule by executive decree undermines human rights and thereby Colombian democracy, while doing nothing to end the armed forces' historical impunity.

The United States government has largely ignored human rights issues in Colombia, despite providing hundreds of millions of dollars in military aid to the Colombian armed forces over the last four years ostensibly for use in the "war on drugs." The lack of end-use monitoring or human rights controls is scandalous given the nature of the equipment transferred, much of it designed for counterinsurgency purposes and provided to forces that have openly declared that their priority is the counterinsurgency war. We call on the United States government to take a visible role in denouncing and controlling abuses committed by U.S.-supported forces, and to withdraw U.S. support should abuses continue.

Peace may not come soon or easily to Colombia. But we agree with Colombia's human rights ombudsman, *Defensor del Pueblo* Jaime Córdoba Triviño, that it will be possible to achieve peace only "when human rights are not neglected, abused, or scorned."[6] A commitment by both sides in the conflict to respect human rights and international humanitarian law might enhance the prospects for peace. It would surely alleviate the suffering of countless civilian victims.

---

[5] Interview, Bogotá, March 2, 1993.

[6] *El Tiempo*, "State Strengthening Respect for Human Rights," in *Foreign Broadcast Information Service* (hereafter cited as FBIS), September 17, 1993, p. 28.

PART I

A PANORAMA OF VIOLENCE

President Gaviria's November 1992 declaration of the state of internal commotion capped one of the worst years of political violence in recent Colombian history. Colombian human rights groups registered over 4,100 deaths in political violence in 1992, an increase of nine percent over the 1991 total and a figure comparable to the record of 4,200 set in 1988, following a surge in massacres committed by paramilitary groups. The 4,100 figure for 1992 included several categories of political murder: outright political assassinations by government forces and the guerrillas; so-called "social cleansing" killings of beggars, prostitutes, the homeless, and other "undesirables"; and disappearances.

Together, murders and disappearances accounted in 1992 for approximately two-thirds of the total deaths in political violence. The remaining one-third involved combat deaths in the guerrilla war. Combat deaths in 1992 also rose slightly over previous years, testimony to the quickening pace of the war following the collapse of peace talks between the government and the guerrillas earlier in the year.[1]

The first nine months of 1993 showed no abatement in the incidence of political violence. More than eleven people a day continued to be killed or "disappeared" for political reasons, approximately three in the armed conflict, six in acts of outright repression (political murders and presumably political murders), and one in "social cleansing." That lamentable tally was augmented by an average of one disappearance a day;[2] according to Presidential Counsellor for the Defense of Human Rights Carlos Vicente de Roux, Colombia ranks third in the world in the number of disappearances.[3] Other violations, including torture, remained

---

[1] Comisión Andina de Juristas — Seccional Colombiana (hereafter CAJ-SC), "Evolución de Situación de Derechos Humanos en Colombia, Violencia en Colombia 1970-1992," Table 1, undated.

[2] Interview, CAJ-SC, October 5, 1993; and CAJ-SC, "Autores de Atentados Contra la Vida Por Razones Políticas, Enero-Septiembre 1993," p. 1.

[3] Interview with *El País*, Cali, in "Human Rights Adviser Notes Gravity of Situation," FBIS, September 14, 1993, p. 34.

3

at appalling levels, while the incidence of arbitrary detention, particularly for crimes of "terrorism," increased. We are convinced that the continuing incidence of such high levels of abuse are directly related to the pervasive impunity enjoyed by members of the Colombian security forces for human rights crimes. Despite sometimes vigorous investigative and disciplinary activity on the part of governmental authorities, those who commit abuses are rarely apprehended and punished.

Political violence as a proportion of overall criminal violence in Colombia is relatively small: perhaps twelve—fifteen percent of the total homicides in Colombia in recent years have been politically motivated.[4] Within the category of political violence, however, the role of state agents and paramilitary groups allied stands out. According to the Andean Commission of Jurists — Colombian Section (CAJ-SC), of the political murders in the first nine months of 1993 in which a perpetrator could be identified, approximately fifty-six percent were committed by the army and security forces, twelve percent by paramilitary groups, twenty-five percent by the guerrillas, and seven percent by a group known as the PEPES or by private assassins. Of those abuses attributed to state agents, over seventy-seven percent were committed by the army and eleven percent by the police.[5] The proportionate responsibility for political violence shifted in

---

[4] Interview with Carlos Vicente de Roux, *El País*, and Gustavo Gallón Giraldo, Elena S. Manitzas, Rodrigo Uprimny Yepes, CAJ-SC, "Los Retos de los 90: Derechos Humanos en Colombia," January 6, 1993, pp. 1-2.

Violence is the leading cause of death in Colombia. According to National Police statistics, a record 25,101 people died violent deaths in Colombia in 1992, almost half of them in the cities of Medellín, Bogotá, and Cali. Colombia's murder rate is approximately nine times that of the United States, according to Presidential Counsellor de Roux. Luis Jaime Acosta, Reuters, "Medellín, La Más Violenta," *El Mundo*, March 23, 1993.

[5] CAJ-SC, "Autores de Atentados," pp. 1 and 4.

The 1993 figures reflected an increase in killings by both official forces and the guerrillas. The comparable statistics for the first nine months of 1992 were: 50 percent by state agents, 33.5 percent by paramilitary groups, 13.2 percent by the guerrillas, and less than one percent by drug-traffickers. CAJ-SC, "Human Rights in Colombia, 1992," January 1993, p. 1 (document submitted to the United Nations Commission on Human Rights). The CAJ-SC noted that the overall percentages could change if drug traffickers were deemed to be responsible for some of the killings that

1993, due to an intensification of the war and an increase in targeted and indiscriminate violence by members of the Medellín drug cartel as well as by insurgent forces. According to official figures (which are no doubt under-estimates), for example, approximately 800 policemen lost their lives in 1992 at the hands of drug-traffickers and guerrillas. The figure for January to May 1993 was over 230, a slight decrease.[6]

The figures compiled by Colombian human rights groups, demonstrate exactly the opposite of what is claimed by the Colombian government and echoed by the U.S. Embassy and State Department; the figures demonstrate that state agents and the paramilitary groups that operate with state acquiescence are responsible for the bulk of the killing. The Colombian and U.S. governments, meanwhile, place the majority of the blame for human rights abuses on the guerrillas and drug traffickers. While we do not wish to diminish the seriousness of guerrilla abuses or downplay the headline-grabbing brutality of the drug cartels, we find that the official characterizations of Colombia's human rights problem are a gross distortion. They serve to obscure the armed forces' preeminent responsibility for Colombia's human rights nightmare and serve to mask the widespread failure to prosecute and punish those responsible for abuses against civilians.

As we have reported in the past, the victims of political violence represent a cross-section of Colombian society;[7] the multiple perpetrators of abuse have contributed to what Presidential Counselor Carlos Vicente de Roux has called a "macabre democratization" of political killing.[8] Targets include peasants living in zones of military conflict, members of

---

took place in undetermined circumstances.

The PEPES (People Persecuted by Pablo Escobar) carried out acts of private vengeance against escaped drug lord Pablo Escobar and his associates and relatives. (See below, The Drug War)

[6] "Asesinados 1,089 Policías en 29 Meses," *Nuevo Siglo*, June 2, 1993.

[7] Americas Watch, *Political Murder and Reform in Colombia: The Violence Continues* (New York: Human Rights Watch, 1992), pp. 1-7.

[8] Interview with *El País*, Cali, in FBIS, September 14, 1993, p. 34.

leftist political parties, trade unionists, human rights activists, members of the judiciary, ex-guerrillas who have laid down their weapons, those killed in "social cleansing" campaigns, and soldiers, police, and combatants themselves. Rural peasants constitute the social group suffering the greatest number of assassinations, disappearances, and torture.[9]

In late 1992 and throughout 1993, the Colombian government adopted exceptional measures to deal with violence, measures embodied in the state of internal commotion decrees and subsequent efforts to convert the decrees into permanent legislation. We deal with these measures at length because we believe that they represent the wrong path to social peace in Colombia. Limitations on individual freedom and enhanced powers to a military establishment already renowned for its brutality may temporarily satisfy a thirst for tougher measures to restore law and order. But ultimately, a continued concentration of power in the hands of the executive branch, additional restrictions on due process and civil rights, and a resort to force in general pose dangerous threats to Colombian democracy. Exceptional powers invite abuse, arbitrariness, and corruption, ills which pose equal, if less immediate threats to the Colombian political system. Americas Watch does not underestimate the dangers to democracy posed by drug trafficking cartels or the guerrilla insurgents. But it should be the government's primary task to ensure that the remedy is not worse than the affliction.

THE DECLARATION OF THE STATE OF INTERNAL COMMOTION

The decrees announced by Gaviria in November 1992 and the extensions of emergency powers at ninety-day intervals throughout the first eight months of 1993 marked a rupture, if not definitive break, in Colombia's process of democratic opening and inclusionary politics. Although one of Latin America's oldest nominal democracies, Colombia

---

[9] Centro de Investigación y Educación Popular (CINEP), "Violencia Política Enero-Diciembre de 1992: Perfiles de las Víctimas, Sector Social," mimeo, January 1993.

has been ruled for thirty-five of the last forty-two years under a state of siege.[10] But beginning in 1990, and in response to a popular initiative, Colombians from across the political spectrum organized to debate and draft a new Constitution to replace the one in effect since 1886. Running parallel to and eventually contributing to this process was a dialogue with insurgent groups that began in the early 1980s and culminated in 1990 and 1991 with the demobilization of three guerrilla groups.[11] The subsequent election of numerous former guerrillas to the Constituent Assembly drafting the new Constitution broadened participation beyond traditional elites and helped cement constitutional human rights guarantees.

The political opening in the early 1990s coincided with a partial abatement of violence carried out by drug trafficking cartels. Drug lords who had unleashed an unprecedented wave of terrorism and violence in the late 1980s — assassinating presidential candidates and declaring open war on Colombia's citizenry — took advantage of new provisions of the Constitution that barred extradition to foreign countries for the purpose of standing trial. Important traffickers turned themselves in to Colombian authorities in exchange for reductions in their sentences. The most notorious of the drug kingpins to surrender was Pablo Escobar, leader of the Medellín cartel, who in June 1991 entered a prison he had personally designed on the outskirts of his hometown of Envigado, Antioquia, outside

---

[10] Gustavo Gallón Giraldo, Elena S. Manitzas, Rodrigo Uprimny Yepes, "Los Retos de los '90," p. 10.

[11] A peace process carried out in the 1980s by the government and the guerrillas secured the demobilization in 1990 of the M-19 guerrilla group. Other negotiations were successfully concluded in 1991 with the dominant faction of the *Ejército Popular de Liberación* (Popular Liberation Army or EPL), the *Partido Revolucionario de los Trabajadores* (Revolutionary Workers Party or PRT), and the Indian-based *Quintín Lame*.

Several groups, however, refused to lay down their weapons. The *Fuerzas Armadas Revolucionarias de Colombia*, or FARC, is the oldest and largest guerrilla group still waging war against the government. Others are the *Unión Camilista-Ejército de Liberación Nacional* (Camilist Union-National Liberation Army or ELN) and a small breakaway faction of the EPL. In 1990, these three groups came together to form the *Coordinadora Guerrillera Simón Bolívar* (CGSB). See Americas Watch, *Political Murder and Reform in Colombia: The Violence Continues*, pp. 49-58.

Medellín. Sixteen months after a prison escape in July 1992, Escobar was killed by the security forces.

Now, however, what Colombian analysts have called the period of *distensión*, or expansion of political space, has come to a close.[12] The declaration of the state of internal commotion in November 1992 and the wave of emergency decrees issued in its aftermath marked a reversion to authoritarian patterns of rule by which power was concentrated in executive hands and governance carried out by executive decree. There are notable restraints on presidential power, embodied most prominently in the Constitutional Court, which was established in 1991 to ensure that decrees issued during a state of emergency were consistent with constitutional protections. The Court has provided important protection against arbitrariness and illegality. But it has been unable to reverse an overall trend toward the weakening of protections guaranteed in the Constitution.[13] (See below.)

The immediate impetus for Gaviria's declaration of the state of exception November 8, 1992, was the November 7 killing of twenty-six policemen in the southern province of Putumayo by the *Fuerzas Armadas Revolucionarias de Colombia* (Revolutionary Armed Forces of Colombia, or FARC). The assault, along with guerrilla bombings in urban areas and relentless attacks on a major oil pipeline leading to the Caribbean coast, took place in the context of renewed guerrilla offensives following a breakdown in May 1992 in peace talks with the government. As discussed later in this report, the guerrilla offensive embodied major and catastrophic violations of international humanitarian law.

The November guerrilla attacks represented yet another in a series of frustrations and set-backs for the government in 1992. In March Colombians learned that drastic power shortages and rationing of electricity

---

[12] Interviews, Bogotá, February 28, March 1 and 2, 1993.

[13] Andean Commission of Jurists (Lima), "Two Years Into the New Constitution," *Andean Newsletter*, No. 80, Lima, July 26, 1993, p. 2.

were connected not only to a severe drought but also to massive corruption involving the construction of a state hydroelectric plant.[14]

On July 22, 1992, a little over a year after he had surrendered to Colombian authorities, drug lord Pablo Escobar defied a government order that he be transferred to another prison and walked out of the jail he had effectively controlled during his incarceration. The day of the transfer, Escobar took National Prison Director Col. Hernando Navas Rubio and Assistant Justice Minister Eduardo Mendoza as hostages and slipped away with nine fellow prisoners. Escobar's escape was made possible by corrupt prison guards and army soldiers surrounding the prison, and marked a serious defeat for the government's policy of negotiating the surrender of drug traffickers.[15] Subsequent revelations — that Escobar's posh jail was equipped with a bar, kitchenette, big-screen television, jacuzzi, fax machines, computers, and cellular telephones,[16] that the conditions of his confinement were known to government officials, and that he had continued to direct drug trafficking operations and order assassinations from his jail cell — all humiliated the government, which mounted an intense man-hunt to track Escobar down.[17]

---

[14] In August 1993 thirty-five government officials investigated for irregularities and cost over-runs at the Guavio hydroelectric plant were acquitted following an investigation by the Procuraduría. *Actualidad Colombiana* (a publication of CINEP, Instituto Latinoamericano de Servicios Legales Alternativos [ILSA], and Colombia-Hoy Informa), No. 137, August 18-31, 1993, p. 1.

[15] Marc Chernick, "Escobar's escape plagues Colombian president," *Latinamerica Press*, November 5, 1992, p. 4; CAJ-SC, "La Situación de Derechos Humanos en Colombia: Compleja Pero No Confusa," September 17, 1992, p. 2.

[16] Inravisión Televisión Cadena 1, "Prosecutor General Reports on Envigado 'Resort,'" FBIS, August 4, 1992, pp. 23-24; Mary Speck, "Bar, Jacuzzi: Welcome to Pablo Escobar's Cell," *Miami Herald*, August 11, 1992.

[17] Within weeks of Escobar's escape, the Ministry of Defense forced into retirement three senior military officers overseeing prison security: Lt. Col. Hernando Navas, director of the prison system, Lt. Col. Manuel José Espitia Sotelo, commander of the military police battalion guarding the prison, and Gen. Gustavo Pardo Ariza, head of the Fourth Brigade based in Medellín. Acting Air Force Commander Gen. Hernando Monsalve resigned following criticism that he delayed

If Gaviria's popularity sank to new lows by the end of 1992 — an opinion poll conducted by Colombia's leading newsweekly magazine *Semana* showed overall approval ratings at just twenty-two percent in January 1993, down from seventy-nine percent a year earlier[18] — attitudes toward the guerrillas also hardened. Egregious violations of international humanitarian law, including summary executions, attacks in urban areas, kidnapping for ransom, and economic sabotage causing massive ecological damage, reaped a whirlwind of public hostility. In November 1992, dozens of prominent writers, journalists, lawyers and academics led by Nobel Prize-winning novelist Gabriel García Márquez wrote an open letter to the Simón Bolívar Guerrilla Coordinator (CGSB) charging that "your war, understandable in its origins, now runs against history....

Kidnapping, coercion, extortion, which today are your most fruitful instruments, are at the same time abominable violations of human rights. Terrorism, which you yourselves always condemned as a legitimate form of revolutionary struggle, is now a daily occurrence. Corruption, which you reject, has contaminated your own ranks, through your dealings with drug trafficking....The innumerable needless deaths from both sides, the systematic attacks on national wealth, the ecological disasters, are costly and undeserved taxes for a country that has already paid so much.[19]

---

authorizing planes to ferry in additional troops following Escobar's escape.

An investigation by the Attorney General's office released in late November 1992 called for charges to be brought against at least 100 army officers, Justice Ministry personnel, and prison officials. The report criticized ex-Justice Ministers Jaime Giraldo and Fernando Carrillo, both of whom had directed the surrender policy and authorized security arrangements at the Envigado prison. Mary Speck, "3 more ousted for bungling Escobar security," *Miami Herald*, July 28, 1992; Andean Commission of Jurists (Lima), "Pablo Escobar's Escape," *Drug Trafficking Update*, No. 32, December 7, 1992, p. 6.

[18] Cited in Douglas Farah, "Escape of Escobar Dims Bright, Shining Colombian Presidency," *Washington Post*, February 24, 1993.

[19] Text, letter to the Coordinadora Guerrillera Simón Bolívar, November 20, 1992.

Growing disenchantment with the guerrillas, even by previously-sympathetic intellectuals, merged with overall exhaustion with violence in general. Together they created a strong reservoir of public sympathy for tougher government measures to reestablish order. Thus, according to a survey conducted by the *El Tiempo* newspaper, when President Gaviria declared the state of emergency, only twenty-one percent of those polled thought the measures went far enough.[20]

FROM STATE OF EMERGENCY TO TOTAL WAR

In his November 9, 1992, President Gaviria lashed out at "the terrorists, murderers, and kidnappers, against that handful of deranged fanatics who have not read in the newspapers the sorry story of the end of communist totalitarianism," and announced a series of financial, military, and political measures to combat the guerrillas.[21] The speech and the measures outlined in it appear to have two roots: 1) a decision by the government beginning in 1990 to commit significant new resources to the armed forces, as part of a multi-faceted effort to end the guerrilla insurgency; and 2) the breakdown of peace talks between the guerrillas and the government in mid-1992 amidst a sea of mutual recriminations. By late August 1993, the government's confidence in the military strategy and lack of faith in guerrillas' desire for peace was so complete that Defense Minister Rafael Pardo Rueda ruled out future peace talks with the major rebel groups. "We do not believe there is need to modify the strategy and policy to restore public order," Pardo said following the funeral for thirteen policemen killed in an August 1993 attack by the FARC. "Instead, we must strengthen and intensify them."[22]

---

[20] Don Podesta, "Colombians Lash Out at Violence," *Washington Post*, December 6, 1992.

[21] Bogotá radio and television networks, "Gaviria Address to the Nation," FBIS, November 9, 1992, pp. 34-36.

[22] Inravisión Televisión Cadena 1, "Defense Minister Rules Out Talks with Rebels," FBIS, August 31, 1993, p. 24.

11

President Gaviria described the contours of the government's security policy in a speech the day before he declared the state of emergency.

> For two years we have been strengthening the army's capacity, creating new mobile brigades, professionalizing the soldiers who face the guerrillas, improving the salaries of the troops and officers, bolstering military intelligence, and significantly increasing the resources of the Colombian armed forces.[23]

So-called "war taxes" were first assessed in 1991 via levies on oil, coal, and nickel exports as well as on international phone calls and domestic electric consumption. Additional surtaxes on income and oil exports were announced by the Finance Ministry in mid-March 1992, designed to generate some $210 million in additional funds for the military budget.[24] According to Minister of Defense Pardo, the funds were used "to create several mobile counterguerrilla groups, battalions, and brigades" made up of professional soldiers that had completed their military service and re-enlisted, receiving additional training.[25] According to official figures, between 1990 and 1992 the number of professional soldiers increased from 2,000 to 12,000; by 1993 the number rose to 15,000. Between 1991 and 1993, the number of professional police increased by 8,000. Twenty-two new Anti-Extortion and Kidnapping Units (UNASE), elite units of police and army officers specializing in the freeing of kidnap victims, were also created during the 1991-1993 time period.

---

[23] Bogotá Radio and Television Networks, "Gaviria Addresses Nation, Calls for Unity," FBIS, November 9, 1992, p. 33.

[24] Notimex, "Military to Increase Budget by $210 Million," FBIS, March 16, 1992.

[25] El Nuevo Siglo, "Defense Minister Rafael Pardo Interview," FBIS, December 14, 1992, p. 51. The Colombian press reported in November 1993 that only two of the four army divisions had their own anti-guerrilla brigade. The goal was, within two years, to have an anti-guerrilla brigade in each army division, to augment the work of the Mobile Brigades and the twenty-five anti-guerrilla companies. El Tiempo, "Armed Forces Modernization Plan Outlined," FBIS, November 8, 1993, pp. 61-62.

Overall, defense spending in 1993 was two-and-a-half times what it was in 1990, whereas it had already doubled between 1980 and 1990. Gaviria proposed adding 140 billion pesos (approximately $185 million) to the defense budget in 1993, in order to add 6,000 more professional soldiers and 4,000 professional policemen.[26] In early August 1993, the government issued an emergency decree to add 64.2 billion pesos (about $84.6 million) to the budgets for the Defense and Justice Ministries, to cover a deficit created when the Constitutional Court declared illegal the government's attempt to issue mandatory war bonds to increase defense spending.[27]

The beginning of the precipitous increase in the size of the Colombian military coincided precisely with the moment of greatest success in peace negotiations with the guerrillas. The dual strategy of negotiating while expanding the armed forces reflected the government's determination, in Defense Minister Pardo's words, "not to put all its eggs in one basket."[28] Another major component of the government's effort to defeat the guerrillas was the plowing of new resources into the judiciary, particularly

---

[26] During the 1990-1993 period, Gaviria said that social spending had quadrupled and spending on the judiciary had tripled. Bogotá Television and Radio Networks, "Gaviria Address to the Nation," FBIS, November 9, 1992, p. 36; Inravisión Televisión Cadena 1, "Gaviria Gives Speech on Antiterrorist Measures," FBIS, February 24, 1992, p. 24; "$160 Mil Millones Para la Seguridad Nacional," El Tiempo, February 23, 1993; Edgar Téllez and María T. Ronderos, "Seguridad y Defensa: Una Década Perdida," El Tiempo, February 14, 1993.

Conversions between pesos and dollars are based on the average yearly official exchange rate as reported in International Monetary Fund, International Financial Statistics (Washington, D.C.: International Monetary Fund, November 1993).

[27] El Tiempo, "Funding Approved to Cover 'War Bond' Gap," FBIS, September 14, 1993, p. 38.

[28] Notimex, "Military to Increase Budget by $210 Million," in FBIS, March 16, 1992, p. 34.

Similarly, Gaviria said that "the dialogue the national government has been holding with the CGSB does not exhaust its peace policy; the dialogue is only one of the policy's components." El Nuevo Siglo, "Gaviria Letter on Prospects of Peace Talks," in FBIS, April 29, 1992, p. 28.

into the special court jurisdictions set up to deal with crimes of drug trafficking and terrorism. (See below)

In 1993, however, the government appeared bent on a new stage of confrontation *without* dialogue in order to finish off the guerrillas. The armed forces' confidence in the possibility of military victory appears to be prompted by the collapse of communism in the Soviet Union and Eastern bloc, and the conviction that, in Gaviria's words, the guerrillas "no longer represent any ideals...they only seek the enrichment of their leaders and the growth of checkbooks based on kidnappings, extortion, hired assassins, and protection money."[29]

The guerrillas bear a large measure of responsibility for the breakdown of the peace talks in 1992, as noted by Presidential Counselor Horacio Serpa when he resigned on September 30, 1992 as head of the governmental peace commission. The March 1992 kidnapping of former government minister Argelino Durán and his death while in guerrilla custody caused an indefinite suspension of the peace dialogue on March 31, 1992. New rounds of talks, scheduled for May and October, never got under way, due to irreconcilable demands made by both sides: the government, for an immediate ceasefire, and the guerrillas, for immediate discussion of socio-economic and human rights issues. Important divisions within the guerrilla movement and within the FARC in particular, over the desirability of a negotiated solution fueled the stalemate.[30] In mid- to late-1993, the government engaged in fitful preparations for talks with the *Corriente de Renovación Socialista* (Socialist Renovation Current), a dissident faction of the ELN, but the talks were suspended after the deaths of two CRS spokesmen in late September in circumstances suggesting army responsibility.[31]

---

[29] FBIS, November 9, 1992, p. 35.

[30] Interview, Colombian political analyst who requested anonymity, Bogotá, March 1, 1993.

[31] In mid-December 1993 the Procuraduría instituted charges against seven officers and enlisted men of the army's Voltígeros Battalion for abuse of authority, negligence, and cover-up in the murders of the two CRS spokesmen. The Procuraduría also recommended an investigation of Presidential Counselor for Peace

14

The guerrillas clearly do not shoulder all of the blame for the failure of the dialogue; in fact, according to CRS leaders, their spokesmen were murdered in cold blood while concentrating troops who, with government knowledge and approval, were about to lay down their weapons. The existence of sectors of the government hostile to peace talks was confirmed by Peace Counsellor Serpa, who condemned in his resignation letter "a war-like stance within the government that hasn't been dealt with. To talk about closing off all options, except that of a war, is wrong."[32] Indeed, army and armed forces commanders Generals Hernán José Guzmán and Ramón Emilio Gil Bermúdez, respectively, declared openly in July 1993 that military measures were the only alternative to defeat subversive groups and pacify the country.[33]

Such a strategy would be less troubling were it not for the systematic abuses, described in this report, by the very elite troops being thrown into battle against guerrilla insurgents. Newly-created counterinsurgency units and Mobile Brigades have been responsible for massive human rights violations against the civilian population living in conflict zones, including indiscriminate attacks, murder, torture, the destruction of property, and arbitrary arrest and incarceration. Furthermore, despite governmental assurances that substantial resources have been channeled into the judicial system in order to punish abuses and speed up trials of those detained, we see no sign that there is a will on the part of the armed forces to prosecute those who have committed human rights violations, in order both to punish the perpetrators and to set an example that abusive behavior is not to be tolerated. The civilian justice system has proven no more successful in

---

Ricardo Santamaría and one of his assistants for failing to adopt measures that would minimize the risk to the CRS spokesman. Procuraduría General de la Nación, Press Release, December 13, 1993, pp. 1-3; Andean Commission of Jurists (Lima), "A New Opportunity for Peace," *Andean Newsletter*, No. 79, June 1993, pp. 2-4; *Actualidad Colombiana*, "Torpedeado Proceso de Paz con la CRS," No. 139, September 14-28, 1993, pp. 3-5.

[32] Andean Commission of Jurists (Lima), "Head of Peace Commission Resigns," *Andean Newsletter*, No. 71, October 1992, p. 4.

[33] Inravisión Televisión Cadena 1, "Armed Forces, Army Commanders Voice Opposition to Dialogue with Guerrillas," FBIS, July 12, 1993, p. 42.

prosecuting human rights cases involving the army and security forces. Impunity remains the principle obstacle to long-term improvement in the human rights situation.

IMPUNITY

Colombia's political system counts with an extensive civilian apparatus to investigate human rights cases, publicize findings, initiate disciplinary and criminal proceedings, and carry out education and advocacy on behalf of human rights. A *Consejería Presidencial para la Defensa de los Derechos Humanos* (Presidential Counselor for the Defense of Human Rights) advises the president on human rights matters, responds to public inquiries, and conducts human rights education and training within the armed forces and other branches of government. A *Procuraduría General* (General Prosecutor) investigates misconduct by government officials, including human rights violations by members of the armed forces; the Procuraduría can issue disciplinary sanctions, the most severe of which is dismissal. The newly-created office of the *Fiscal General* (Attorney General) conducts criminal investigations and prosecutions, notably in the volatile areas of drug-trafficking and terrorism.[34] The Office of the *Defensor del Pueblo*, or human rights ombudsman, was also created by the 1991 Constitution. It has taken over much of the case work previously undertaken by the Presidential Counselor on Human Rights, and its Complaints Office (*Oficina de Quejas*) serves as a key point of contact between civilian victims of abuse and the government.

Despite this impressive infrastructure, prosecutions of those who commit human rights crimes are extremely rare. A report released in October 1992 by the *Defensor del Pueblo*, for example, documented 717 cases of murder of elected officials, candidates, and members of a small

---

[34] The office of the *Fiscal* was created by the 1991 Constitution. The current Attorney General, Gustavo de Greiff, is a widely-respected figure who has been personally touched by drug-related violence. De Greiff's daughter resigned her position as Minister of Justice when drug traffickers threatened to kill her children. Douglas Farah, "Colombia's Official Crime Buster," *Washington Post*, February 15, 1993.

16

leftist party, the *Unión Patriótica* (Patriotic Union or UP), between the party's founding in 1985 and September 1992.[35] The Defensoría attributed the majority of the killings (306 out of 717) to paramilitary groups, and a high percentage to the army and police (129 out of 717). Despite the pervasive persecution of members of the UP, however, the report demonstrated that a judicial sentence had been reached in only ten of the 717 cases. (Six cases were acquittals and four were convictions.)[36] The Defensoría noted that the height of the killings coincided with major UP electoral successes, and occurred despite a government pledge in 1985 to provide the "indispensable guarantees and security" necessary for full participation in the political life of the country.[37]

There are numerous obstacles to accountability in Colombia, but one of the most serious is a provision of the 1991 Constitution granting military court jurisdiction in cases involving military personnel, and the extension of that *fuero militar* to the police. Moreover, the Constitution sanctifies the defense of "due obedience" to higher orders, allowing subordinates to

---

[35] Defensor del Pueblo, "Estudio de Caso de Homicidio de Miembros de La Unión Patriótica y Esperanza, Paz y Libertad," Informe para el Congreso, el Gobierno, y el Procurador General de la Nación, Santafé de Bogotá, October 1992, pp. 1-172.

The Unión Patriótica (UP) was founded in May 1985 as a result of a process of dialogue between the government of President Belisario Betancur and the FARC. In the first elections in which it participated, the UP gained five Senate seats and nine seats in the House of Deputies. Also elected were fourteen departmental deputies, 351 town council members, and twenty-three municipal mayors.

The UP itself places the number of victims of political murder from within its ranks at over 2200.

[36] The report also documented the murder of 113 demobilized rebels belonging to the EPL guerrilla group between January 1991 and September 1992. Most of those responsible for the murders were listed as unknown (sixty-eight cases) while a dissident wing of the EPL which refused to lay down its arms was deemed responsible for twenty-one deaths. Defensor del Pueblo, "Estudio de Caso de Homicidio," pp. 70, 69, and 124.

[37] Ibid., p. 36.

claim innocence on the grounds that they were acting on orders of a superior officer. We know of few cases in which military courts have sentenced officers or soldiers for human rights abuses, and even fewer for which the punishment is commensurate with the crime.

In 1992, for example, members of the army's "García Rovira" battalion who had murdered eleven peasants in the municipality of Macaravita, Santander, in June 1990 were acquitted by a military court. The Procuraduría supported an appeal, based on its own investigation linking members of the military to the crime. But the acquittal was confirmed in December 1992 by a 2d War Council (court martial).[38]

Other well-known cases in which military courts have acquitted members of the armed forces, even though there was ample documentation of their participation in human rights abuses, are the 1987 murder of Sabana de Torres mayor Alvaro Garcés Parra,[39] and the 1991 murders of seventeen civilians in Los Uvos, Cauca, who were pulled off a public bus

---

[38] Asociación SETA, *Misión de Identificación de Derechos Humanos en Colombia, Informe de Misión*, May 1993, Brussels, Belgium (report prepared at the request of the Commission of the European Community, External Relations Directorate), p. 59.

The killings took place in the context of a military offensive against the ELN. Following the killings, the army closed off the site and later presented the bodies dressed in military-style uniforms. The day after the murders, Col. Alfredo Rodríguez Velandia of the V Brigade in Bucaramanga reported that nine guerrillas had been killed in combat. See Americas Watch, *The "Drug War" in Colombia: The Neglected Tragedy of Political Violence* (New York: Human Rights Watch, 1990), p. 62; and Americas Watch, *Political Murder and Reform*, p. 38.

[39] Two army officers, Major Oscar Echandía Sánchez and Captain Luis Orlando Ardila Orjuela of the Ricaurte Battalion, provided a gun permit and official identification card to a gunman who attacked and killed Garcés. The gunmen, one of three attackers, was killed in a shootout with the mayor's bodyguards. Three of Garcés's bodyguards also perished. The Procuraduría found the two military officers responsible for preparatory acts to murder and requested their dismissal. In October 1989, however, the military court of the 5th army brigade acquitted them of all charges. A military appeals court (*Tribunal Superior Militar*) upheld the lower court decision. One of the officers eventually retired from the armed forces and another was, in fact, dismissed. See Defensor del Pueblo, "Estudio de Caso de Homicidio," pp. 145-149; and Americas Watch, *Political Murder and Reform*, p. 21.

18

and executed on the spot. The army originally blamed the guerrillas for the Los Uvos massacre (see below).

Occasionally, criminal proceedings against members of the military have been initiated by the *Fiscal General*, or Attorney General, in the civilian justice system, on the grounds that human rights abuses are equivalent to acts of terrorism.[40] In general, however, criminal proceedings in these courts have tended to languish and have resulted in few convictions.

The 1992-1993 period saw important setbacks in some of the disciplinary proceedings initiated by the Procuraduría. In the past, we have noted that the effectiveness of the institution has been determined in large measure by the people who have occupied important posts. We are pleased to reaffirm our admiration for the work of the Procuraduría's Office of Special Investigations (OIE), whose committed staff have researched and documented the facts in important cases and have vigorously pressed for sanctions of those responsible for abuses. Unfortunately, we cannot say the same for the Procuraduría's former Delegate for the Armed Forces, César Uribe Botero, who stated in a public communiqué that his term had been successful in that only 1.7 percent of cases resulted in military discipline.[41] According to representatives of the European Community who investigated human rights in Colombia in early 1993, Uribe told them

If military court jurisdiction [*fuero*] is not respected, the decisions of ordinary judges could become a tool that destroys the bulwark of democracy, which is the military forces...The enemies of the Colombian democratic system will say that there have to be daily

---

[40] In 1984 and 1987, Colombia established so-called public order courts to try cases of drug-trafficking and terrorism. The courts, now called *jueces regionales* or regional judges, are presided over by "faceless judges" whose identities are concealed to protect them from reprisal. The courts allow for secret witnesses and secret testimony, and involve serious restrictions on due process rights for defendants. See below, and Americas Watch, *Political Murder and Reform*, pp. 98-105.

[41] Andean Commission of Jurists (Lima), "Worrying Impunity," *Andean Newsletter*, No. 77, April 1993, pp. 3-4.

dismissals, in order to weaken the army and our pluralistic democracy.[42]

We are troubled that such a key official within the Procuraduría appeared to share the military's view that human rights prosecutions were a guerrilla strategy aimed at undermining the armed forces and sapping morale. We are suspicious, moreover, of the enthusiasm regarding the role of the Procuraduría expressed by commander of the Colombian armed forces General Ramón Emilio Gil Bermúdez. Whereas senior military leaders had complained in the past of a "Procuraduría syndrome" in which the military felt persecuted by civilian overseers, Gil Bermúdez declared in March 1993 that "from an institutional standpoint, relations are great now."[43] The following summary of some important cases may reveal the source of Gil Bermúdez's enthusiasm.

Urabá

In March and April 1988, paramilitary operatives backed by military officers murdered twenty banana workers on the Honduras and La Negra plantations in Antioquia province. Procuraduría Delegate for the Armed Forces César Uribe asked for the dismissal of three members of the Army's 10th Airborne Brigade, Lt. Colonel Luis Felipe Becerra Bohórquez, Capt. Vicente Bermúdez Lozano, and Sgt. Félix Antonio Ochoa Ruiz.[44]

According to the Procuraduría, these three officers and their troops had searched the farms the month prior to the massacre, without a judicial warrant and accompanied by heavily-armed civilians. Several people suspected of collaborating with the guerrillas were captured during the

---

[42] Asociación SETA, *Misión de Identificación de Derechos Humanos en Colombia*, p. 59.

[43] *El Tiempo*, "Armed Forces Commander on Guerrillas," FBIS, March 4, 1993, p. 39.

[44] At the time of the massacre, Becerra was a major, Bermúdez was a 2nd lieutenant, and Ochoa was a corporal.

sweep and one detainee apparently named other alleged guerrilla sympathizers that were then systematically eliminated.

The Procuraduría found that the three members of the Airborne brigade had actively collaborated in the massacre by supplying the assassins with the names of suspects, by providing the hitmen with classified information, and by permitting the presence of armed civilians in the original search. Moreover, according to the Procuraduría, the three officers had information that the massacre was being planned and did nothing to stop it.[45]

On April 20, 1993, however, the Procuraduría Delegate for the Armed Forces acquitted all three officers of responsibility, citing a lack of evidence that would link the officers to the massacre. (The review team did conclude that there was evidence pointing to the participation of members of the army.)[46]

Americas Watch has not reviewed the documentation gathered in the Procuraduría's original investigation, and therefore cannot comment on its quality. But we are deeply concerned that the "lack of evidence" rationale has long been used by the military itself to clear soldiers and officers of involvement in horrendous crimes. Moreover, we are dismayed at the attitude of the armed forces, which during the investigation not only promoted all three officers under investigation but also sent one of them, Lt. Col. Becerra, to the United States for training.[47] Meanwhile, a military court acquitted the officers of responsibility for the Urabá killings, a decision which has been appealed before the Superior Military Tribunal.

---

[45] Major Becerra had also allegedly used his credit card to pay for the hotel stay of civilians who executed the massacre. Procurador General Carlos Gustavo Arrieta told Americas Watch in December 1993 that this proved to be false.

Military courts that claimed jurisdiction over the case deemed that the role of the officers was only "dereliction of duty" because they had failed to prevent the murders, despite other evidence of their more direct participation in acts preparatory to murder. Americas Watch, *Political Murder and Reform in Colombia*, pp. 19-21.

[46] Hernando Valencia, Procuraduría Delegada para la Defensa de los Derechos Humanos, letter to Americas Watch, November 11, 1993, p. 1; *Actualidad Colombiana*, No. 128, April 14-27, 1993, p. 4.

[47] Americas Watch, *Political Murder and Reform*, p. 20.

The Urabá case demonstrates that even those cases which have received wide national and international attention will end in impunity for members of the armed forces.[48]

The consequences of that impunity were tragically illustrated in late 1993, when troops of the Palacé Battalion commanded by Lt. Col. Becerra massacred thirteen civilians in Riofrío, Valle. According to eyewitnesses, hooded men broke into the home of the Ladino family in the early morning hours of October 6, torturing and murdering seven family members ranging in age from fifteen to seventy-five years. Several of the women victims were raped. Four members of the Molina family and a girlfriend of one of them were also dragged from their home and shot. Another civilian who arrived with the squad was executed. The office of the Procuraduría announced an investigation, while Lt. Col. Becerra insisted that his troops killed armed guerrillas of the ELN, charges that were echoed by the commanders of the III Army Division and III Army Brigade.

On November 10, 1993, presumably in response to the international outcry over the Riofrío killings, Lt. Col. Becerra was removed from active duty.

Trujillo

The outcome of the investigation of the disappearance, torture, and murder of twenty-six people from the town of Trujillo, Valle, in 1990 represents a serious miscarriage of justice.[49] Many of those abducted and killed appear to have been involved in a conflict with local landowners, who went to the army, accusing the squatters of belonging to the ELN guerrillas.

---

[48] By contrast, two paramilitary leaders, Henry de Jesús Pérez and Fidel Castaño, were convicted *in absentia* 1991 in for their role in planning the Urabá massacre. Pérez was killed later that year in an apparent feud between paramilitary leaders. Fidel Castaño remains at large. (See below, section on the drug war, for Castaño's alleged participation in ongoing paramilitary violence.)

[49] For background on the case see Americas Watch, *Political Murder and Reform*, pp. 34-36.

In September 1991, a Public Order court acquitted five civilians, including two members of a paramilitary group, of any involvement in the crime. Over a year later, on December 22, 1992, the Procuraduría acquitted several police and army officers of any responsibility for the murders. Army Major Alirio Antonio Urueña Jaramillo of the "Palacé" Battalion had been linked to the crime by an employee of the landowners, who testified that he saw some of the victims murdered with a chain saw. (The employee "disappeared" after returning to Trujillo without protection,[50] and a second witness received a death threat and refused to continue cooperating with the court.)

Citing a lack of evidence, the Procuraduría acquitted Major Urueña; then-Commander of the Third Police District of Tuluá, Major Alvaro Córdoba Lemus; the head of police intelligence (F-2) of Tuluá, Sgt. Luis Aníbal Alvarez Hoyos; and the police commander of Trujillo, Lt. José Fernando Berrío Velásquez.[51] There appear to be no other criminal or disciplinary proceedings under way in connection with this atrocious massacre.

El Nilo

In mid-December 1991, some fifty heavily armed men, hooded and in military style uniforms, violently attacked a community of Páez Indians on the "El Nilo" farm near Caloto, Cauca. Twenty people were killed, some after being bound and forced to lie on the floor. Speculation at the time as to a motive for the killings focused on a land dispute between the indigenous community and the desire of drug traffickers to use the land for poppy cultivation to produce heroin.[52]

---

[50] He had been declared insane by the Institute of Legal Medicine in Bogotá after being examined in the presence of army doctors.

[51] "'Locura' en Fallo Sobre Massacre," *El Espectador*, January 8, 1993; Hernando Valencia, letter to Americas Watch, November 11, 1993, p. 1. For a critique of the decision, see Justicia y Paz, letter to Carlos Gustavo Arrieta Padilla, August 25, 1993, pp. 1-7.

[52] Americas Watch, *Political Murder and Reform*, pp. 31-34.

Following the appointment of a high-level investigative commission, and a visit to the site by President Gaviria himself, seven perpetrators of the massacre were identified and five arrested. Some of those detained reportedly identified members of the National Police, including a major, as involved in the murders. Two lawyers were murdered and an anthropologist "disappeared" in early 1992; all of them had been investigating the case.

In February 1993, and based on an investigation by the Procuraduría's Office of Special Investigations, the Procuraduría's Delegate for Human Rights issued charges against Major Jorge Enrique Durán Argüelles, police commander of the Second District of Santander de Quilichao, and Captain Fabio Alejandro Castañeda Mateus, commander of the anti-narcotics company of that unit. The Procuraduría said that the two officials, "along with personnel of the National Police under the command of the Captain and of civilians Orlando Villa Zapata, Leonardo Peñafiel, Edgar Antonio Arévalo Peláez, and Nicolás Quintero Zuluaga, went to the [El Nilo] hacienda and proceeded not only to destroy and burn the dwellings of the Indians but also opened fire indiscriminately, causing the deaths of twenty Indians."[53] On July 8, 1993, however, the Procuraduría's Delegate for Human Rights absolved the two officials of any wrongdoing, claiming a lack of proof that the two were material authors of the crime. Incredibly, the new Delegate for Human Rights Hernando Valencia, wrote Americas Watch that "the report of the Office of Special Investigations was not adequately and sufficiently taken into account in the disciplinary decision."[54]

---

[53] "Dos Oficiales Implicados en Masacre de Indígenas," *La Prensa*, February 12, 1993; Colectivo de Abogados "José Alvear Restrepo," "Resúmen de Casos," undated, p. 5.

[54] Hernando Valencia Villa, Procurador Delegado para los Derechos Humanos, letter to Americas Watch, November 11, 1993, p. 2.

In August 1993, the human rights ombudsman (Defensor del Pueblo) formally requested that the Procuraduría reconsider its July ruling.[55] A panel of three senior Procuraduría officials, including the head of the Office of Special Investigations, was commissioned to review the record. The panel split, however, and presented two reports on September 14, 1993. The majority opinion was that there was insufficient evidence that the two police officers actually participated in the crime, and that charges should have been brought for cover-up and omission.[56]

The penal investigation of the case, meanwhile, has been marred by delays and laxity. The *Fiscalía Regional* based in Cali failed to order the preventive detention of Major Durán and Captain Castañeda, a decision that was upheld at the appeals level (*Tribunal Nacional*) after a challenge by the Procuraduría. Investigators of the Procuraduría's Office of Special Investigations have noted other irregularities in the conduct of the criminal court, including the release of a principal civilian suspect and allegations by court officials that denunciations of the massacre were a "show" put on by guerrilla groups to discredit the National Police.[57]

Los Uvos

In April 1991, armed gunmen stopped a public bus in the Department of Cauca, pulled seventeen passengers from the vehicle, and executed them on the spot. The commander of the local army battalion in Piedrasentada, Lt. Col. Paulo Alfonso Briceño Lovera, blamed the murders on the guerrillas, and later brought legal action for "defamation" against a

---

[55] Procuraduría General de la Nación, Procuraduría Delegada para la Defensa de los Derechos Humanos, Resolución No. 008 de 1993, July 8, 1993, pp. 1-44; Amnesty International, Urgent Action, AMR 23/51/93, August 31, 1993, p. 1.

[56] Hernando Valencia, letter to Americas Watch, p. 2.

[57] Procuraduría General de la Nación, Oficina de Investigaciones Especiales, Expediente No. 134918, undated, pp. 282-284; Colectivo de Abogados, "Resúmen de Casos," p. 6.

Colombian human rights group that accused the army of carrying out the killings.[58]

In May 1993, however, the Procuraduría opened disciplinary proceedings against eight members of the "José Hilario López" army battalion for murder and cover-up of the Los Uvos killings. Corporals José Gustavo Mora Parra, Miguel Antonio Gil Orozco, Pedro López Gamboa and José Agustín Cañón González were named as material authors of the crime. Three senior officers were named for covering up the actions of their subordinates: Battalion Commander Col. Paulo Alfonso Briceño Lovera, second in command Major Manuel Rodríguez Díaz Granados, head of the Third Section Major César Augusto Saavedra Padilla, and 2d Lt. José Edilberto Cortés Valero.[59]

The Procuraduría once again signalled deficiencies in the penal investigation carried out by military courts, suggesting that disciplinary proceedings be initiated against three officers: Commander of the Third Army Brigade General Víctor Arévalo Pinilla, his judicial assistant, Antonio José Bolívar Cardona, and the judge of the 19th Penal Military Court, Major Alvaro Ochoa Barrera. The military court had ruled that members of the José Hilario López Battalion were not responsible for the massacre.[60]

Fusagasugá

In August 1991, army assailants murdered five members of the Palacios family and two other men, entering the Palacios's house at 2:45

---

[58] The National Coordinating Body for Human Rights, Victims and Refugees of Colombia (CONADHEGS) sent investigators to the scene and interviewed a witness who implicated the army. 7.62 mm bullet casings, the kind used by the Colombian army, were also reportedly found at the scene. The case brought by Briceño was later dropped. See Americas Watch, *Political Murder and Reform*, p. 27; and Amnesty International, "Killings in Cauca Department — Army Officially Accused," May 1993, p. 2.

[59] "Cargos a 8 Militares," *El Espectador*, May 19, 1993.

[60] *Actualidad Colombiana*, No. 128, April 14-27, 1993, pp. 4-5; Amnesty International, "Killings in Cauca Department," p. 2.

a.m. and executing all seven on the spot. Those murdered included a sixty-five-year-old activist of the Unión Patriótica, two of his children, and his son-in-law. The day of the killings, the army issued a communiqué claiming that it had killed seven members of the FARC in a confrontation. Commander of the army XIII Brigade, General Jesús María Vergara Aragón, publicly insisted on that version of the events in days subsequent to the killings.[61]

Within a month of the killing, Military Court No. 115 ordered the arrest of eight soldiers, including Second Lieutenant Tomás Emilio Cruz Amaya and Second Sergeant William Ramírez Roa, accused of commanding the operation in which the civilians were killed. After being held for 120 days, the two were granted provisional liberty. Military court proceedings have continued at the Logistical Support Brigade.

In March 1993, the Procuraduría ordered the dismissal of Cruz Amaya and Ramírez, and ordered the suspension for thirty days of Lt. Col. Víctor Manuel Bernal Castaño, who participated in the coverup.[62] Six months after it was ordered, the Ministry of Defense carried out the suspension of Lt. Col. Bernal Castaño.

UNASE

In February 1993 the Procuraduría issued indictments against 150 members of the special anti-kidnapping and anti-extortion units UNASE, including two colonels, five lieutenants, and one captain of the police as well as four army officers. The officers and more than 100 soldiers based in Medellín were accused of kidnapping, torturing, and "disappearing" civilians.

---

[61] The events were characterized as "a confrontation in which seven subversives belonging to the XXV Front of the FARC were killed." A statement from the XIII Brigade confirmed "the deaths of seditious ones in Fusagasugá. The victims, fully identified, had arms, munitions, and dynamite." Defensor del Pueblo, "Estudio de Caso de Homicidio," pp. 133-135; Americas Watch, *Political Murder and Reform*, pp. 25-27.

[62] "Piden Destituir a Tres Militares," *Nuevo Siglo*, March 26, 1993.

The indicted members of UNASE engaged in the very practices they were supposed to stop. According to press reports, kidnappers who were apprehended by UNASE were tortured to find out the whereabouts of their victims. Once the information was verified, the kidnappers were made to "disappear." Members of the UNASE unit then transferred the original kidnap victim to another location, and contacted the victim's family to demand ransom to be paid to the members of UNASE. Family members of kidnappers were also abducted by UNASE, in order to exchange them as hostages.[63]

The investigation into UNASE was carried out jointly by the Procuraduría and the *Departamento Administrativo de Seguridad* (DAS). It was opened when a pilot belonging to a kidnap ring escaped, handcuffed and wounded, from his UNASE captors and told his story to the local Procuraduría office in Medellín.[64] The investigation remains at the initial stages.

In April 1993, a governmental commission composed of the Presidential Counselor for Human Rights, human rights ombudsman, Procurador General, and members of the Red Cross was formed to look into additional charges that members of UNASE investigating the kidnapping of journalist Jaime Ardila of *El Espacio* were involved in the death of an Arsario Indian and the disappearance of eight others.[65]

Senior Military Involvement with Paramilitary Groups

In November 1992, the Procuraduría issued formal charges against seven senior military officers for their illicit involvement with paramilitary groups in the Department of Santander. The highest ranking officer

---

[63] Leslie Wirpsa, "Colombian Vigilantes Join Hunt for Pablo Escobar," *Latinamerica Press*, March 18, 1993, p. 1; "Cargos a Miembros de UNASE," *El Espectador*, February 19, 1993.

[64] Ibid., and Emisoras Caracol, "Attorney General Indicts UNASE Personnel," FBIS, February 22, 1993, p. 25.

[65] Radio Cadena Nacional, "Commission to Investigate Complaint Against UNASE," FBIS, April 28, 1993, p. 40.

indicted was Brig. Gen. Carlos Gil Colorado, former head of the Fifth Brigade and currently head of intelligence for the army general command. Three captains and three lieutenants were also charged. According to the Procuraduría, the officers permitted the operations of such paramilitary groups as the "San Juaneros" (the Guys from San Juan), the "Tiznados" (the Blackened Faces), the "Mano Negra" (Black Hand), the "Grillos" (the Crickets), the "Pájaros" (Birds), the "Caracuchos," and the "Masetos." Paramilitary agents were allowed to participate in military operations and to use military helicopters to transport arms. The officers also helped set up military bases that were subsequently left in the hands of private individuals belonging to paramilitary groups.[66]

THE REPORT OF THE PROCURADURÍA

Colombia's grim human rights record was challenged in June 1993 by the Procuraduría in its second public report, which minimized abuses committed by the state in 1992.

The Procuraduría reported having opened 2,618 new cases in 1992 representing 3,099 victims, including those killed in seventy-four massacres, 403 homicides, 370 disappearances, 232 cases of torture, 634 cases of personal injury (*lesiones personales*), 618 arbitrary detentions, 212 illegal searches, 249 threats, and 307 other complaints. Although the occupation of most victims (2,062) was not known, of those who were identified, the most were peasants, followed by businesspeople.

In one of its most incisive critiques, the report admits that the majority of the staggering number of victims apparently had no connection to a political party, union, or other organization. However, they were *perceived* by state agents as not being independent, but rather, as forming part of a "collective enemy."

[The security forces] act under the premise that gained currency in El Salvador, of 'draining the sea,' which means that a direct relationship

---

[66] "Pliego de Cargos Contra Siete Oficiales Del Ejército," *Nuevo Siglo*, November 18, 1992.

is established, for example, between trade union or peasant movements and the subversive ranks. When counter-guerrilla actions are carried out, these passive subjects are not identified as 'independent' victims, but rather, as part of the enemy.[67]

The report distinguishes between military and ideological enemies, saying that "tacit or explicit sympathies do not make an individual or a group a military enemy."[68]

Fifty-eight percent of the complaints involved the National Police.[69] Both the DAS and the Judicial Police registered far lower numbers of abuses, although the DAS was the only force implicated in a higher number of cases as compared to 1991. By contrast, the Judicial Police registered a seventy percent drop in complaints. The report offers two hypotheses for why this might be so: either its agents wear civilian dress and therefore are not identified as members of the force when abuses are committed, or its incorporation in 1992 into the Attorney General's office provided more effective civilian oversight.[70]

Overall, the Procuraduría concluded that police were responsible for two murders a week in 1992 and one wounding every ten days; all of these cases involved the illegal use of arms. The report scored the command structure of the police for "despotism," "unnecessary hardness and tyranny," and "intimidation," and said that the predominant image of the police was that of "the repressor."[71] Of the 1,000 disciplinary charges issued against the police (representing seventy-three percent of all charges issued by the Procuraduría in 1992), sixty percent resulted in punitive

---

[67] Procuraduría General de la Nación, *Informe Sobre Derechos Humanos*, June 1993, p. 28.

[68] Ibid., p. 29.

[69] Ibid., p. 43. The police were also themselves a major target of political violence.

[70] Ibid., pp. 31-34.

[71] Ibid., pp. 53 and 47.

action, the vast majority against low-ranking officers or agents. Most were related to arbitrary detention and personal injury, defined by the Procuraduría as physical harm that falls short of torture.[72]

Slightly less than sixteen percent of the complaints registered by the Procuraduría involved the armed forces, a surprisingly small number given the large portion of abuses attributed by human rights groups to the military.[73] Of the 191 disciplinary charges filed against members of the armed forces, however, only twenty-four resulted in sanctions, most against mid-level officers. Most of the sanctions involved cases of massacre, homicide, disappearance, or torture, grave violations reflecting a

> *modus operandi* of the armed forces, according to which those agents involved in violations of human rights, by virtue of their training for war, have the tendency to attack the right to life and integrity [of the person] more than liberty: [the armed forces] tend not to use intimidatory or dissuasive tactics, but rather opt to eliminate those they consider the enemy.[74]

The departments with the highest number of reported human rights violations by state agents were Santafé de Bogotá, the capital; Antioquia, Santander (particularly the Urabá region) and Norte de Santander, which form part of the Middle Magdalena region; and the Cauca Valley. Among municipalities, the case of Barrancabermeja (Santander), considered the capital of the Middle Magdalena, stands out. In 1992 seventy complaints

---

[72] Ibid., pp. 47-51.

The prevalence of police abuses led the Colombian government to form a Commission for the Reform of the National Police, composed of representatives from the Procuraduría, Fiscalía, Defensor del Pueblo, and Comptroller's office.

[73] See above, A Panorama of Violence.

[74] Ibid., pp. 40 and 42.

were received by the Procuraduría, more than triple the number of the second-ranking municipality.[75]

Despite the report's impressive attempt to document the breadth of human rights violations in Colombia, we find several major problems with its interpretations. The report begins by arguing that the view that both the state and armed groups violate human rights can now be considered "hegemonic," and that among all armed groups, the state is the only one whose legitimacy "is beyond doubt." Therefore, it is "the one that violates human rights the least."[76]

This assertion errs in its interpretation of international law, which holds that only states can violate human rights, while armed insurgents can violate the laws of war and international humanitarian law by committing certain acts, such as the killing of non-combatants or attacks against civilian targets. In this context, the concept of "legitimacy" demands that the state recognize, respect, and protect the human rights of its citizens, a responsibility other armed groups do not share. "Legitimacy" does not allow the government greater latitude in committing abuses, or to attempt to justify, as this report does, abuses that occur out of a supposed overzealousness in the defense of democracy. It, in fact, puts a greater burden on the state, which in the case of Colombia has yet to be fully assumed.

Furthermore, the report tends to absolve the military high command of responsibility for both human rights violations and impunity, arguing that abuses are committed by mid-level officers acting independently. This claim is difficult to defend given the military's structure and mode of operation, and absolves senior officers of responsibility for the actions of their subordinates, itself a grave problem if it leads to human rights violations.[77] Moreover, although the Procuraduría asserts that government authorities made a great effort in recent years to improve Colombia's human rights record — an effort which we acknowledge — the horrifying

---

[75] Ibid., pp. 10-16.

[76] Ibid., p. 4.

[77] CAJ-SC, "El Informe sobre Derechos Humanos de la Procuraduría General de la Nación," August 1993, pp. 5-6.

statistics, reports, and testimonies of victims gathered by independent human rights groups attest to a grimmer reality.

The report mentions that fewer than ten percent of the complaints it receives eventually become full-scale legal cases, but fails to analyze on a deeper level why this is so.[78] One of the reasons appears to be that investigators, particularly from the office of the Procurador Delegate for the Armed Forces, often did not carry out serious, in-depth inquiries, shelving complaints after only cursory reviews, or with glaring errors in procedure, or in apparently blatant disregard of available evidence. Of the decisions taken in 1992, seventy percent were to shelve cases with no resolution, in effect an acquittal of those implicated.[79]

At issue as well is the fear that prevents many from formalizing complaints to a government office, something which undoubtedly leads to an underrepresentation of abuses.[80] On repeated occasions Americas Watch has received reports that individuals who have made complaints or who transmitted them to the Procuraduría (*personeros*,[81] for example) have suffered threats and attacks subsequently. These obstacles to reporting get short shrift in the report. In addition, we have received disturbing reports that the paperwork for some investigations linked to complaints by

---

[78] Procuraduría General de la Nación, *Informe Sobre los Derechos Humanos*, p. 5.

[79] Ibid., p. 55.

[80] Based on the data it gathered, the report concluded that the majority of abuses take place in urban rather than rural areas, a finding consistent with the naming of the National Police as the principal abuser of human rights. The rural/urban split may have more to do, however, with the relative difficulty of lodging a complaint in the countryside and the risks associated with doing so.

[81] A *personero* is a local ombudsman appointed by municipal authorities, to insure that authorities, including the police and military, heed the Constitution and obey the law. They receive complaints from the citizenry about official abuses and transmit them to the Procuraduría for investigation. However, they have no authority to emit sanctions.

civilians of indiscriminate bombings and aerial strafing by the military have been misplaced, leaving the cases in a kind of bureaucratic limbo.[82]

The most serious failure of the report, however, is the lack of any assessment of the efficacy of sanctions — whether state agents found guilty by the Procuraduría of having committed abuses are ever actually punished. This analysis was also missing from the 1991 report, the Procuraduría's first. Reliable sources have indicated that, of the cases in which the Procuraduría recommends disciplinary sanctions, about thirty-five percent of the sanctions are ignored. This appears especially to be true in the case of the armed forces.

To its credit, the Procuraduría report does highlight some of the difficulties it faces when investigating allegations, particularly those that involve the military. For instance, the Procuraduría attributed its failure to produce more sanctions to the

> deep-rooted *esprit de corps*, badly interpreted by some of its members, which results in a notorious lack of solidarity with the investigator, unable to gather information in the quickest and most reliable form because of cover-ups, complicity, or simply the silence of fellow officers or those implicated.[83]

High-ranking army officers have frequently criticized the Procuraduría for fomenting a sense of fear among field officers, who they claim are restricted in their operations because of the threat of eventually being investigated and sanctioned (a phenomenon known as the "Procuraduría syndrome"). To these assertions, Procurador General Gustavo Arrieta has responded firmly and with courage, insisting on respect for human rights, and in his view, making progress in changing military attitudes.[84]

Although there is much room for improvement in the way cases are investigated and resolved within the Procuraduría, it must be said that more

---

[82] Justicia y Paz, letter to Americas Watch, July 1993.

[83] Procuraduría General, *Informe Sobre Derechos Humanos*, p. 39.

[84] Interview, Procurador General Carlos Gustavo Arrieta, December 1, 1993.

complaints are making their way to the disciplinary phase than three years ago, perhaps due to the Procurador's vocal defense of human rights and his stated commitment to serious, in-depth investigations. In addition, with the opening of special Human Rights Offices in Medellín, Bogotá, Cúcuta and Cali (with another one planned for Barrancabermeja), the Procuraduría is making an effort to make the act of lodging a complaint easier and less risky for civilians.

IRREGULAR USE OF THE "PUBLIC ORDER" COURTS

Since 1989, Americas Watch has reported on the development and practices of special court jurisdictions established to hear cases involving drug-trafficking and terrorism.[85] Currently known as *jurisdicción regional* at the trial level and *Tribunal Nacional* at the appellate level, these special court jurisdictions are more commonly referred to as the "public order" courts, their name under legislation passed in 1988. The courts were created because of the high incidence of murderous attacks on judges and judicial officials, particularly by drug traffickers, and the conviction that insurgents and drug traffickers posed such a danger to society that exceptional means were needed to combat them. Between 1979 and 1991, for example, the Andean Commission of Jurists — Colombian Section documented 515 cases of violence against judges and lawyers, including 329 homicides and attempted homicides.[86]

But the courts, from their inception, have involved such severe restrictions on defendants' due process rights that the jurisdiction itself is an invitation to serious abuse. The identity of judges is concealed by use

---

[85] For the evolution of these courts, see Americas Watch, *The Killings in Colombia* (New York: Americas Watch, 1989), pp. 93-98; *The "Drug War" in Colombia: The Neglected Tragedy of Political Violence* (New York: Human Rights Watch, 1990), pp. 92-97; and *Political Murder and Reform in Colombia: The Violence Continues* (New York: Human Rights Watch, 1992), pp. 98-105.

[86] International Commission of Jurists and Andean Commission of Jurists — Colombian Section, *Justice for Justice: Violence Against Judges and Lawyers in Colombia, 1979-1991,* (Bogotá: CAJ-SC, July 1992), p. 1.

of one-way mirrors and special microphones which distort their voice; this measure, while providing some sense of protection, also does away with a sense of personal accountability, itself necessary to ensure impartiality.[87] The public order jurisdiction also permits the use of secret prosecution witnesses and testimony, making it impossible for the defense to cross-examine a witness or challenge an accuser's credibility. At times, the secret witness is him or herself a member of the intelligence services.[88]

In practice, defense lawyers have little or no access to the court files until the trial stage; at times, they have no access whatsoever. In addition to making it next to impossible to mount an adequate defense, this limits the challenging of evidence during the investigative stage, something that is possible in Colombia's ordinary justice system. Pre-trial release is severely restricted, as is the possibility for *habeas corpus*. Petitions to have a case dismissed because of violations of due process can only be presented at the sentencing stage, after the presumption of guilt is well entrenched.[89]

Predictably, tilting the balance of power so dramatically in favor of the prosecution led to the temptation to use the public order jurisdiction in an overly zealous fashion. Beginning in mid-1992, Colombian human rights groups demonstrated that the overwhelming majority of cases heard by the public order courts involved cases of non-violent social protest having

---

[87] Americas Watch, *Political Murder and Reform*, p. 103.
We do not wish to imply, however, that no "faceless" judges are impartial. Americas Watch has met *fiscales* within the public order system and was impressed by their integrity and dedication.

[88] CAJ-SC, letter to Americas Watch, October 27, 1993, pp. 2-3.

[89] An executive decree, converted into permanent legislation in 1992, provided that habeas corpus for public order offenses could only be presented before the *fiscal* hearing the case. Previously, the petition could be presented before any judge. Interview, CAJ-SC, October 5, 1993; CAJ-SC, letter to Americas Watch, October 27, 1993, pp. 1-2; CAJ-SC letter to Robert K. Goldman, October 27, 1993, p. 1.
For a summary of the criticisms of the public order courts, including additional cases identified by the Colectivo de Abogados "José Alvear Restrepo," see Lawyers Committee for Human Rights, "Lawyers Committee's Concerns With the Public Order Courts in Colombia," preliminary report, October 1993, pp. 10-20; and Comisión Intercongregacional de Justicia y Paz, "Las Injusticias de la Justicia Colombiana," *Justicia y Paz*, Vol. 6, No. 2, April-June 1993, pp. 5-19..

nothing to do with guerrilla insurgency or narcotrafficking. According to a study by CINEP, only six percent of the 2,648 cases adjudicated in the public order system since its creation involved terrorism.[90] In addition, many of the cases of drug trafficking involved peasant cultivators of coca, individuals at the lowest rungs of the drug trade who only with difficulty could be construed as a threat to judicial officials. During a February 1993 visit to La Uribe, Meta, Americas Watch was also able to confirm a number of cases in which peasants living in areas where the guerrillas were active were also subjected to the public order jurisdiction, thrown into jail on trumped-up charges by the military of being auxiliaries of terrorism. (See Part II of this report.)

Among the most celebrated of the cases reflecting the abuse of the public order jurisdiction was that of the *Empresa Nacional de Telecomunicaciones* (TELECOM) workers. In April 1992, workers in the state telecommunications agency went on strike to protest the privatization of the company. Telephone service was interrupted for approximately one week and the Colombian government declared the strike illegal. Following the strike (during which workers were forcibly evicted from the premises by the National Police and one engineer was murdered in suspicious circumstances), the state company brought charges of sabotage against the union. A criminal court judge, however, determined that the case involved "terrorism" as defined in a state of emergency decree, and passed the case to a public order court.[91]

Between February and April 1993, a prosecuting *fiscal* issued arrest warrants for sixteen workers, thirteen of whom were captured or turned themselves in and were subsequently held, without bail, in Bogotá's

---

[90] Diego Pérez, "Des-Orden Público," *Cien Días*, Vol. 5, No. 19, July-September 1992, pp. 28-29.

[91] The decree stipulated sentences of ten to twenty years in prison for those who "provoke or keep the population or part of it in a state of turmoil or terror, through acts that pose a danger to life, the physical integrity or freedom of persons, buildings, or means of communication, transport, processing or flow of fluids or energy, by application of means capable of causing extensive damage."

Modelo prison.[92] Possibly as a result of sustained national and international pressure, the case was transferred back to the ordinary courts on November 2, 1993 and the charges reduced to "disrupting telecommunications." The 13 workers were provisionally released after some eight months in jail.

The vast majority of cases, however, have less happy endings. In October 1993, the CAJ-SC released the preliminary results of an investigation into due process and other violations in the public order system. They identified numerous cases involving trade unionists, peasant leaders, and opposition politicians charged under anti-terrorist statutes, thereby confirming a pattern of the criminalization of social protest. Some of those charged were being held solely on the basis of testimony by secret witnesses.[93] The liberal application of the public order jurisdiction against social critics of the government stands in stark contrast to the near-total failure of the public order system to prosecute terrorist crimes committed by paramilitary groups or by the security forces themselves.

According the CAJ-SC's study, due process violations — incommunicado detention for more than the 36 hours permitted by the Constitution, arrests without judicial warrant, lack of access to defense counsel, the arrest of civilians by the armed forces without court warrant, interrogations by the security agencies, torture — were rampant. Overall, the CAJ-SC found that the jurisdiction's most common targets were not the dangerous criminals for which it was designed, but rather, vulnerable segments of the population and people of "humble social standing."[94]

While more research is needed to amplify these findings, there is now more than sufficient evidence that the public order courts are not functioning as originally intended. Nor has the system offered complete

---

[92] Interviews, Lourdes Castro and Eduardo Umaña (attorneys for the TELECOM workers), March 2, 1993.

[93] CAJ-SC, "Violaciones a los Derechos Fundamentales de los Procesados por Delitos Adelantados ante la Jurisdicción de Orden Público, Hoy Justicia Regional," Informe Preliminar, October 1993, pp. 5-6 and 9-10.

[94] Ibid., abstract, p. 2.

protection to judges, even though there has been a reduction in attacks.[95] In late October 1993, a non-commissioned officer of SIJIN, a police investigative unit, was charged with preparing attacks against faceless judges at the behest of the Cali cartel, signalling what may be a much wider problem of corruption of judges and others working within the public order system. In September 1992, faceless judge Myriam Rocío Vélez was murdered, allegedly by hitmen associated with drug lord Pablo Escobar. Rocío Vélez was investigating the case linking Escobar to the 1986 murder of journalist Guillermo Cano. In November 1993, Senate Vice President Darío Londoño Cardona was murdered by a group calling itself "Death to Protectors of the Cali Cartel". Londoño had taken a lead role in Congress's passage of a law turning an executive decree dealing with public order issues into permanent legislation.[96] It was widely assumed that the ELN was responsible for the attack.

Misuse of the public order jurisdiction, moreover, has contributed to a choking backlog of cases, undermining one of the system's central rationales — efficiency.[97] In August 1993, Attorney General Gustavo de Greiff indicated that he had 1,431 deputy prosecutors to handle approximately 300,000 cases.[98] Clearly, further steps must be taken to limit the courts' reach only to those who would truly represent a mortal threat to the lives of judicial officials, to remove the armed forces from the gathering of evidence, and to establish more adequate guarantees for the accused.

---

[95] This reduction might have less to do with the anonymity afforded judicial officials than with the government's policy of negotiating the surrender of drug traffickers in exchange for reduced sentences. CAJ-SC, letter to Americas Watch, October 27, 1993, p. 2.

[96] Inravisión Televisión Cadena 1, "Prosecutor General on Military-Cartel Ties, Senator's Death," FBIS, November 8, 1993, p. 58; Notimex, "ELN Claims Responsibility," FBIS, November 8, 1993, p. 56.

[97] Interview, official of the public order courts, March 2, 1993.

[98] He called for the immediate hiring of another 477 deputy prosecutors. *El Tiempo*, "De Greiff Faults Criminal Justice System," FBIS, September 14, 1993.

THE EROSION OF CONSTITUTIONAL GUARANTEES

The urge to resort to extraordinary measures is understandable given the intractability and cruelty of violence in Colombia and the variety of actors involved in it. But severe restrictions on the exercise of democratic freedoms can themselves constitute a kind of time bomb, by leading to arbitrary actions by the state that erode its legitimacy in the eyes of the public.

Decrees promulgated under the November 1992 state of internal commotion, for example, included the following measures:

◆ the assigning of judicial police functions to the armed forces, giving the military unprecedented powers to investigate civilians;

◆ restrictions on broadcast media prohibiting live coverage of guerrilla actions or the airing of guerrilla communiqués or interviews with the insurgents;

◆ additional powers to the police and other security agencies to carry out searches, detentions (*arresto preventivo*), and interceptions of communications without judicial order;

◆ mandatory purchase of "war bonds" for all individuals and corporations whose income in fiscal year 1991 exceeded seven million pesos ($11,000) or whose gross assets were more than thirty million pesos ($47,000);

◆ the suspension of governors or mayors — without any judicial process — who held talks with guerrilla groups without the authorization of the executive branch.

◆ a prohibition on granting pre-trial freedom to any person held for a public order crime.[99]

All told, the government introduced approximately forty emergency measures between November 1992 and May 1993, many of which have been submitted to the Congress for approval as permanent legislation.

A number of the internal commotion decrees were overturned by the Constitutional Court. In February 1993, for example, the Court ruled that the assignment of judicial police powers to the military was unconstitutional. It did state, however, that investigative units working under the direction of the Fiscal could be created within military units, as long the investigators were civilians. The Court's ambiguous ruling leaves open the danger that the Fiscal's control over the new investigative bodies will be in theory only. In practice, the military is likely to exercise more definitive control, to the detriment of civilian rights.

The Court rejected in April 1993 the mandatory purchase of war bonds and ruled that money collected prior to the Court ruling had to be refunded. The Court upheld, however, the executive's power to suspend local officials who held unauthorized talks with the guerrillas, and the prohibition on live broadcasts of guerrilla actions or interviews with the insurgents.[100]

Two additional Court rulings, in May and August 1993, limited judicial powers that the government saw as essential in its war on drug-trafficking and terrorism. In May the Court ruled that it was unconstitutional for the Fiscal General to hold negotiations with criminal suspects or offer reductions in sentences in exchange for cooperation with the judicial system. The Court found that such powers granted to the Fiscal (an executive branch, not a judicial official) undercut the powers of judges. According to the majority of the Court, granting a partial or total reduction

---

[99] CAJ-SC, "Guerra Total en Colombia," December 1, 1992, pp. 1-6; Comisión Intercongregacional de Justicia y Paz, *Justicia y Paz*, Vol. 6, No. 2, April-June 1993, p. 18; interviews, Bogotá, March 1 and 2, 1993.

[100] Inravisión Television Cadena 1, "Court Upholds Internal Disturbance Decrees," FBIS, February 19, 1993, p. 25; Emisoras Caracol, "Constitutional Court Rules War Bonds Unconstitutional," FBIS, April 27, 1993, pp. 30-31.

in the penalty for a crime was a form of pardon, which under Colombian law can only be granted by Congress or by the president (in the case of political crimes). Moreover, the Colombian Penal Procedures Code authorizes judges to decide whether or not to accept a reduction in sentence.[101] The effect of the Court's ruling is not to do away with "plea bargaining" altogether, but rather, to limit the Fiscal's ability to detract from the powers of judges in this area.

In a ruling equally troubling to the Gaviria administration, the Court declared on August 3, 1993, that detainees held for public order crimes could not be deprived of conditional liberty.[102] The ruling affected between 1,600-2,000 of the prisoners considered to be most dangerous and held for drug-trafficking and terrorism offenses.[103] Rather than permit a

---

[101] Interview with Constitutional Court President Hernando Herrera Vergara, Bogotá Emisoras Caracol, "Constitutional Court President Interviewed," FBIS, May 5, 1993, p. 19.

[102] Section 415 of Colombia's Code of Penal Procedures, which took effect in July 1992, stipulates that prisoners can request pre-trial release if formal charges have not been filed after 180 days. Separate provisions, however, covering the public order crimes of terrorism and drug-trafficking, impose much more stringent conditions for pre-trial release. Those provisions state that a prisoner is eligible for pre-trial release only if seventy years old or more, or if the time in jail has exceeded the maximum possible sentence for the crime with which he or she is charged. In issuing its August 1993 decision, the Court avoided taking sides as to which provisions — the Penal Code or decree laws — governed prisoners held for public order crimes. The Court stated, in essence, that prolonged detention without charge was a violation of constitutional rights. *Semana*, August 10, 1993, "Emergency Decree Antecedents Discussed," FBIS, September 16, 1993, pp. 35-36; interview, Gustavo Gallón G., Andean Commission of Jurists — Colombian Section, October 5, 1993.

[103] In a September 1993 ceremony marking national human rights day, President Gaviria stated that approximately 2,000 persons were being held in jail charged with belonging to guerrilla groups. Gaviria announced that the government was developing "close modes of cooperation between the armed forces and the Attorney General's office to bring offenders before judges and defeat them in court."
The total number of prisoners held for public order crimes, however, is much higher, approximately 5,000. The Bogotá newsweekly magazine *Semana* reported in September that there were 5,400 prisoners. *El Tiempo*, "State Strengthening

release of prisoners, and in direct contradiction of the Court's ruling, President Gaviria immediately issued an emergency decree giving judges an additional thirty months in which to file formal charges.[104] The emergency decree demonstrated not only the Gaviria administration's undermining of decisions by the Court, but also that the special courts set up to deal with drug-related crimes and terrorism were, in fact, less efficient than claimed by the government. While Americas Watch is sympathetic to the need to keep notorious criminals behind bars, it deplores the lack of expeditious judicial action, itself a grave violation of due process rights.

THE LAW TO REGULATE STATES OF EXCEPTION

In the first half of 1993, the Gaviria government also re-submitted to the Congress a bill to regulate states of exception, the so-called *Ley Estatutaria Sobre los Estados de Excepción*. A number of its repressive provisions were rightly condemned by Colombian human rights groups as well as by Defensor del Pueblo Jaime Córdoba Triviño. The law as introduced by the executive branch would have: 1) given the government, during an external war, powers to establish internal exile and "zones of confinement" similar to the U.S. internment of Japanese-Americans during World War II[105]; 2) revived the power of military tribunals to judge

---

Respect for Human Rights," FBIS, September 17, 1993, p. 27; *Miami Herald*, August 4 and 5, 1993.

[104] The government had acted in similar fashion in July 1992, invoking, for the first time since the passage of the new Constitution, a state of internal commotion in order to prevent the release of prisoners. The July 1992 action was not widely criticized because the newly-created office of the Fiscal, which itself came into being in July 1992, had not had sufficient time to develop evidence that would result in a formal indictment.

A law passed by the Colombian Congress late in 1993 mandated a six-month investigative period for public order cases.

[105] The U.S. government formally apologized and has paid reparations to the victims of this war-time policy.

civilians in times of foreign war (despite a categorical prohibition in the Constitution); 3) given the armed forces the right to occupy any locale and suspend any activity simply on the suspicion that activities underway would disturb public order; 4) required civilians to give military officials prior notice of any voyage or trip (a form of *empadronamiento*); 5) granted the president power unilaterally to modify penalties for and definitions of what constitutes a crime; and 6) given the security forces the power to carry out detentions, searches, and interception of communications without judicial warrant.[106] Human rights ombudsman Jaime Córdoba Triviño denounced the draft law as a "veiled prolongation of the situation of juridical abnormality" the country was experiencing and sent an eighteen-page document detailing his criticisms to the Congress.[107]

The Senate removed some of the law's most objectionable provisions, including the creation of military courts to judge civilians, zones of confinement, *empadronamiento*, and internal exile. But both the House and the Senate allowed several clearly repressive provisions to survive. Most troubling is the Congress's ratification of the security forces' right to carry out searches, detentions, and interceptions of communications without judicial warrant.[108] This aspect of the law not only devolves extraordinary powers to the military and police and removes a source of protection against arbitrary action, it also invites torture and disappearance during unacknowledged detention.

---

[106] Gustavo Gallón Giraldo and José Manuel Barreto, "La Ley de Los Estados de Excepción y la Vigencia de los Derechos Humanos," CAJ-SC, February 1993, pp. 1-5; Humberto de la Calle Lombana, Ministro de Gobierno, Exposición de Motivos, "Del Proyecto de Ley Estatutaria Sobre los Estados de Excepción," pp. 1-32.

[107] Edison Parra Garzón, "El Gobierno No Juega Limpio," *El Tiempo*, March 22, 1993; Jaime Córdoba Triviño, "Defensoría del Pueblo y Estados de Excepción, Reflexiones en Torno al Proyecto de Ley," *Derechos Humanos*, No. 19, January-March 1993, pp. 7-8.

[108] In cases of extreme urgency, judicial permission can be granted verbally, and in the cases of greatest urgency, no written or verbal order is necessary. These supposed limitations are in reality a farce, as the security forces are left with ultimate discretion over when to request judicial permission.

In addition, the Congress upheld restrictions on the media similar to those decreed under the state of internal commotion, and granted the President the power to modify penalties as well as the definitions of crimes. This latter provision concentrated extraordinary judicial powers in executive hands. It also meant that the President could unilaterally extend the definition of crimes such as "rebellion" to cover not only the taking up of arms but also a broad range of activities considered "subversive" by the government. Americas Watch laments that the Congress has bowed to pressures to limit fundamental freedoms in order to step up the war against terrorism.[109] Eroding rights sets up a vicious cycle in which a freer rein given to government forces leads to excesses, which themselves create new sources of grievance.

A similar kind of contradiction can be seen in the anti-kidnapping law approved by Congress in December 1992 and signed by President Gaviria in January 1993. The law prohibits the payment of ransom, and envisions the appointment of an administrator to oversee the assets of a kidnap victim to make sure that no ransom is paid. The law embodies sanctions for Colombian nationals or foreigners that pay ransom, and offers reductions in sentences to those within kidnapping rings that cooperate with government authorities.[110]

While understandable given the rash of kidnappings carried out by drug traffickers, guerrillas, common criminals, and members of the security forces themselves (see above), Americas Watch shares the criticism of the Procurador General, who argued that the state cannot obligate kidnap victims to sacrifice themselves in order to prevent future kidnappings.[111] In effect, the law penalizes kidnap victims and their families twice, adding

---

[109] As of this writing, the Constitutional Court had still not ruled on the legality of the statute to regulate states of exception. It therefore had not been signed by the President or become the law of the land.

[110] Inravisión Televisión Cadena 1, "Anti-Kidnapping Law Approved; Signatures Pending," FBIS, December 14, 1992, p. 52; and Inravisión Televisión Cadena 1, "Gaviria Approves New Law Against Kidnapping," FBIS, January 21, 1993, p. 32.

[111] Andean Commission of Jurists (Lima), "Anti-Kidnapping Law Questioned," *Andean Newsletter,* No. 80, July 26, 1993, p. 4.

to the anguish of kidnapping a prohibition on efforts to free a loved one and the labeling of those efforts as criminal. The Andean Commission of Jurists has also noted that the law attacks the notion of family, violates the right to equal protection under the law, and contradicts the primacy of individual over state interests.[112] Since overall kidnapping rates had fallen even before the adoption of the anti-kidnapping law, Americas Watch urges that the law be repealed.[113] Several of its provisions, including the criminalization of ransom payments, were, in fact, declared unconstitutional on November 26, 1993.

TUTELA

A innovative way for citizens to gain relief when they believe their rights have been violated came under some fire in late 1992. Known as the *acción de tutela*, this measure, included in the 1991 constitution, allows citizens to file for an immediate judicial injunction against actions or omissions of any public authority that they claim limit their constitutional rights. Courts must then hand down a ruling within ten days.

In the first year after taking effect, close to 7,000 *acciones* were submitted to the courts. Colombia's Constitutional Court, which reviews appeals of lower court decisions on *acciones*, alone receives between fifty to one hundred appeals a day, indicating that the *acción de tutela* has become one of the new constitution's most popular and visible reforms. Among the *acciones* granted was one that prevented a private high school from banning a student who wore make-up, violating her right to an education; one that gave police protection to a member of the UP in Norte de Santander, after he successfully argued that his right to personal liberty

---

[112] Ibid.

[113] According to National Police statistics, kidnappings fell by thirty-three percent between 1991 and 1992, from 1,717 cases in 1992 to 1,136 cases in 1991. According to DIJIN, kidnappings fell another 34.5 percent in the first five months of 1993. *El Tiempo*, "National Police Report on Crime Statistics," FBIS, January 14, 1993, pp. 22-23; and "34.5% ha Disminuido el Secuestro en 1993: Dijin," *El Tiempo*, June 9, 1993.

had been violated by death threats made by the army; and one that ordered medical care for an AIDS patient who had been denied care at a state hospital, thus violating his right to not be discriminated against because of his disease.[114]

Among the *acciones* most important to human rights was the *acción* granted to Justicia y Paz and several individuals who helped the government gather information on paramilitaries and their links to the army's Fifth Brigade in El Carmen, Santander. After a botched effort in March 1992 to arrest twenty-six men implicated in paramilitary activity, priest Bernardo Marín and tailor Orlando Rueda were identified and described in the national press as ELN guerrillas who had supposedly "infiltrated" the Procuraduría, Attorney General's office, and judge's chambers. Justicia y Paz was termed "a guerrilla sympathizer." After energetic protests and a successful use of the *acción de tutela*, Colombia's largest daily, *El Tiempo*, printed a retraction clarifying that Father Javier Giraldo, director of Justicia y Paz, and the two others were not guerrillas or sympathizers. Refusing to honor the court order, *La Prensa* editor Juan Carlos Pastrana spent ten days in jail.[115]

In August, the television station QAP received a list of 150 people and institutions considered by military intelligence to be collaborators or supporters of guerrilla organizations, including human rights workers, trade unionists, and grassroots activists, thereby putting their lives at serious risk. Efforts to prevent its publication included an *acción de tutela* before a Bogotá judge, who ordered QAP and all other media organizations to refrain from publication. The judge also ordered the Defense Ministry to abstain from making public intelligence information on individuals. However, the Defense Ministry appealed and the initial ruling blocking the publication of the list was overturned by the Bogotá Appeals Court in November. In the ruling, the Appeals Court reasoned that given the impossibility of locating the list or establishing the accuracy of the

---

[114] "La tutela pasó el año," *Semana*, November 24, 1992.

[115] "La increíble y triste historia de El Carmen," *El Tiempo*, June 14; Letter to Carlos Gustavo Arrieta, Procurador General, from human rights groups, July 6; Rectifications in *El Tiempo* on July 25, August 4, and October 18; Rectification in *La Prensa* on October 2; "Delfín en la cárcel," *Semana*, May 25, 1993, pp. 58-59.

intelligence on which it is based, it would be legally impossible to protect the constitutional rights of the individuals concerned. As this report went to press, the CAJ-SC was appealing the decision before the Constitutional Court.[116]

Some public officials, including the Procurador General, have criticized an overuse of the *acción* as a potential usurpation of the duties of public officials, in particular judges hearing cases that are suddenly resolved by parallel *acciones*.[117] Some Colombians attempted to use the *acción de tutela* to appeal judicial sentences handed down after trials, which the Constitutional Court determined in October 1992 was not permissible, as it undermined the autonomy of judges. After an intense debate among the Court's seven justices, the majority delineated three exceptions: excessive delay in court decisions, acts by a judicial employee that threaten constitutional rights, and to prevent permanent damage caused by a judicial decision.[118] It remains to be seen whether the Court's October 1992 decision, by limiting the *acción de tutela*, constitutes what one justice called "the first step of the counter-reform" of the new Constitution,[119] or whether the exceptions will prove sufficient to protect citizens' rights.

ATTACKS ON HUMAN RIGHTS MONITORS

Americas Watch reports with great sadness that attacks on our colleagues in the human rights movement accelerated in 1993, product of an attitude within the military equating human rights advocacy with

---

[116] Letter to Americas Watch from CAJ-SC, October, 1993; and Amnesty International Urgent Action 263/93, August 6; and follow-up on November 11, 1993.

[117] "Tutela desplaza a la justicia," *El Espectador*, June 22, 1993.

[118] CAJ-SC, "Admisibilidad de la Tutela Contra Decisiones Judiciales," October, 1993, p. 1.

[119] Quoted in Andean Commission of Jurists — Colombian Section, "Human Rights in 1992," undated, p. 3.

subversion and the complete lack of accountability for previous murders and disappearances of human rights activists. Since our last report, another member of the *Comité Regional para la Defensa de los Derechos Humanos* (CREDHOS) in Barrancabermeja, Santander has been murdered: Julio César Berrío was shot in an ice-cream parlor on June 28, 1992, and later finished off in the street as he tried to flee his assailants. We are aware of no ongoing investigation into Berrío's death. Earlier that month, unidentified gunmen fired on a vehicle carrying CREDHOS director Jorge Gómez Lizarazo and two other CREDHOS workers when they were returning, along with three community leaders, from investigating a massacre. Gómez has since left Colombia for fear of his life.[120]

Those who have courageously tried to continue the work of CREDHOS have also suffered threats and harassment at the hands of the armed forces. In May, June, and July 1993, senior army officers of the Nueva Granada Battalion based in Barrancabermeja verbally attacked CREDHOS workers when they inquired about or tried to visit detainees on the army base. On several occasions, officers, including Battalion Commander Luis Fabio García, accused CREDHOS members of being spokespersons for the guerrillas.[121]

The most serious attack on a human rights monitor in 1993 involved the disappearance of Delio Vargas, president of ASCODAS, an organization assisting the internally displaced population. Vargas was abducted on April 19, 1993 in Villavicencio, Meta, by five armed men in civilian dress. He was forced into a vehicle and has not been heard from since. Vargas, a founder of the *Comité Cívico Por los Derechos Humanos* (Civic Committee for Human Rights) in Meta, was an organizer of a seminar to discuss peace alternatives in the region. The seminar was scheduled to take place four days after his abduction, and human rights workers in the area reported hearing rumors that the armed forces or paramilitary groups would try to sabotage the event. A retired army sergeant and informer for army

---

[120] Gómez's assistant, CREDHOS secretary Blanca Cecilia Valero de Durán, was murdered in January 1992, the day after Gómez published an op-ed in the *New York Times* denouncing human rights abuses by the Colombian armed forces.

[121] CREDHOS letter to Americas Watch, July 1993, pp. 1-8; Amnesty International, Urgent Action, July 19, 1993, AMR 23/42/93.

intelligence was detained in connection with the disappearance but there has been no further action on the case.[122]

Throughout 1993 prominent human rights figures were subjected to threats and harassment connected with their work. In April, attorney Eduardo Umaña Mendoza, lead counsel on the TELECOM case described above, received four anonymous phone calls threatening him with death if he did not cease his activities.[123] In May, a shadowy paramilitary group calling itself the Association for the Defense of Military Honor threatened unspecified measures against human rights groups that published "distorted information" about the armed forces.[124] In August, Rafael Barrios Mendivil, attorney in the Los Uvos and El Nilo cases discussed earlier, received telephone death threats and was followed by agents of the security forces.[125] Barrios subsequently left the country.[126]

Also in August, a Bogotá television station received a list of 150 individuals and groups, including those who work in human rights, who were considered by the military to be guerrilla agents or sympathizers. A Bogotá judge ordered the station not to air the names of those identified,

---

[122] CINEP, "Acción Urgente," April 20, 1993; Justicia y Paz, letter to Americas Watch, May 7, 1993; Mariana Escobar, Consejería Presidencial para los Derechos Humanos, letter to Americas Watch, June 2, 1993.

[123] Amnesty International, "Urgent Action," April 22, 1993, UA 126/93; Lawyers Committee for Human Rights, "Lawyer to Lawyer Network," May 1993.

[124] The group was formed apparently in response to the publication in Europe of *El Terrorismo de Estado en Colombia*, a detailed examination — by anonymous authors — of the human rights record of military officers. On the basis of information in the book, the German government prevented four senior Colombian army officers from entering Germany in early May. *El Espectador*, "Autodefensa del honor militar," May 10, 1993.

[125] Colectivo de Abogados "José Alvear Restrepo," letter to Americas Watch, August 1993.

[126] The office of the Presidential Counselor for Human Rights filed complaints with the Fiscalía, Procuraduría, and DAS so that they would investigate the threats. Carlos Vicente de Roux, Consejero Presidencial para los Derechos Humanos, letter to Americas Watch, November 9, 1993.

a decision overturned following an appeal by the Ministry of Defense. The case was still pending before the Constitutional Court in late November 1993.[127]

These kinds of attacks and threats occur in the context of continued verbal assaults against human rights monitors by the highest echelons of the armed forces. In a September 1993 interview with the Colombian press, Military Forces Commander Ramón Emilio Gil Bermúdez described the work of a human rights monitor based abroad as part of a guerrilla propaganda effort. That same month, Commander of the II Division Major General Harold Bedoya Pizarro lodged a criminal complaint with the Fiscalía against the Permanent Committee for the Defense of Human Rights and dozens of other human rights and political figures; he said their publication of an advertisement calling for the release of imprisoned trade unionists amounted to defamation.[128] Americas Watch views these statements not only as unwarranted attempts to restrict freedom of expression in Colombia, but also as dangerous distortions of the work undertaken by human rights groups. As in the past, we call on the Colombian government to affirm its support for the legitimate and important efforts of human rights groups, to protect those engaged in such activities, and to punish with the full weight of the law those who attack the defenders of human rights.

THE DRUG WAR

Sixteen months after his escape from prison humiliated government officials, Pablo Escobar was hunted down in Medellín by troops of the elite 3,000-man Bloque de Búsqueda (Search Bloc) and killed on a rooftop as he

---

[127] See above, section on the *acción de tutela*.

[128] The ad, said Bedoya, implied that the army carried out arbitrary detentions. Edgar Torres and Clara Elvira Ospina, "Por Qué el Optimismo de los Militares?" *El Tiempo*, September 19, 1993; and "Denuncian a Comité de los D.H.," *El Espectador*, September 7, 1993.

tried to evade his captors.[129] Escobar's death ended one of the most intense manhunts in Colombian history, and closed one of the bloodiest, albeit far from final chapters in the drug war. Even if Escobar's death likely spelled the end of the Medellín drug trafficking cartel, it is unlikely to put a dent in the cocaine trade overall, or eliminate the murderous violence associated with the drug trade.

If Escobar's July 1992 escape from prison represented a major set-back for the government's policy of negotiating the surrender of drug traffickers, it also resulted in merciless waves of renewed violence, much of it aimed at civilians. Escobar declared open war on Colombian society to retaliate for government blows against his organization and to force a renewed agreement over his surrender. Police and army troops executed numerous key Escobar associates, while others surrendered. And two new paramilitary organizations emerged dedicated to Escobar's capture or elimination. One of them, known as the PEPES (for People Persecuted by Pablo Escobar) murdered Escobar's associates and destroyed property belonging to him and his relatives. The lull in drug-related violence that accompanied the passage of the 1991 Constitution which barred extradition was thus abruptly shattered in 1993, injecting more fear and uncertainty into the lives of ordinary Colombians.

Violence following Escobar's prison break escalated notably in September 1992, when cartel hitmen began systematically picking off policemen in Medellín and murdered "faceless" judge Myriam Rocío Vélez, thirty-eight, responsible for linking Escobar to the 1986 murder of *El Espectador* publisher Guillermo Cano. Attacks on the police grew more fierce in October and November, following police operations that resulted in the deaths of key cartel leaders Brance Muñoz Mosquera (alias "Tyson") and security chief Jhonny Edison Rivera Acosta (alias "El Palomo").

---

[129] Escobar, in hiding in Medellín, apparently made a telephone call on a cellular phone to his wife and children in Bogotá. Monitoring equipment provided by the United States reportedly picked up Escobar's voice and led police to him. James Brooke, "Drug Lord Is Buried as Crowd Wails," *New York Times*, December 4, 1993.

Rivera Acosta was one of the nine who had escaped with Escobar.[130] Cartel hitmen assassinated over thirty police in the first two weeks after Muñoz's death alone.[131]

By the end of 1992, some sixty policemen from Medellín had been killed. One year after Escobar's escape, the Bloque de Búsqueda, a combined army and police force dedicated to Escobar's apprehension, admitted to 120 deaths during offensive operations against Escobar and other members of the Medellín cartel.[132] All of the nine inmates who had escaped with Escobar had either surrendered to Colombian authorities or been killed by October 1993.

Police tactics themselves contributed to the spiral of violence, as troops showed little interest in taking prisoners alive. Asked whether he preferred taking Escobar dead or alive, the head of the search bloc, DIJIN Col. Hugo Martínez, stated publicly that he preferred to kill Escobar.[133] U.S. officials expressed sentiments akin to relief that the Colombian troops who

---

[130] Muñoz Mosquera had been charged with murder in connection with the 1989 bombing of an Avianca airliner in which over 100 civilians died. Muñoz was killed in a shootout with dozens of police officers who surrounded his hideout in Medellín. Associated Press, "Airline bomber is killed," *Washington Times*, October 29, 1993.

[131] Inravisión Televisión Cadena 1, "Measures Reduce Murder of Police Agents," FBIS, November 24, 1992, p. 40.

[132] Mary Speck, "Escobar vows to form guerrilla army," *Miami Herald*, January 19, 1993; "Medellin Cartel Report," *Washington Post*, July 19, 1993; El Nuevo Siglo, "Search Bloc Operations, Results Detailed," FBIS, October 28, 1993, pp. 45-46.

[133] Alma Guillermoprieto, "Exit El Patrón," *New Yorker*, October 25, 1993, p. 78.
Those who turned themselves in included Escobar's brother Roberto and John Jairo Velásquez (alias "Popeye"), a top cartel enforcer. Alfonso León Puerta (alias "Angelito"), believed to have managed personal security for Escobar, was killed by police on October 6, 1993, in Medellín. He was the last of those who escaped to be killed or to surrender. Puerta reportedly supervised squads of assassins directed by the cartel. "Top Drug Lord Aide Is Slain in Colombia In a Police Shootout," *New York Times*, October 8, 1993; Andean Commission of Jurists (Lima), "The solitude of the Mafioso," *Drug Trafficking Update*, March 1993, pp. 4-5.

killed Escobar had returned fire rather than open it.[134] Meanwhile, Tahí Barrios, former delegate for human rights in the office of the Procuraduría, stated to a reporter that "I can't tell you how many serious rights violations are being carried out [in the search for Escobar]: illegal raids, arrests, and killings."[135]

Cornered and reeling from the deaths of key cartel operatives, Escobar unleashed a wave of terrorist bombing attacks in early 1993 against civilian targets in major cities. The purpose, as in the past, was to force Colombian society to pay the price for governmental efforts to hunt him down. Between January 21 and 31, 1993, four different car bombs exploded in Bogotá and Medellín, killing twenty-one civilians, including at least five children, injuring scores of others, and resulting in millions of dollars of property damage. Two additional car bombs detonated in a busy downtown area of Bogotá on February 15, 1993, killing four more people and wounding 120. Scores of offices, hotels, and businesses were also damaged.[136] Another bomb that ripped through a car shop in Barrancabermeja in mid-February killed nineteen and wounded twenty, apparently going off prematurely and intended for the cities of either Bucaramanga or Bogotá.

Escobar's deadly escalation of force spawned yet another round of vigilantism, this time by the so-called PEPES. The PEPES launched their organization on January 31, 1993, torching a country chalet belonging to Escobar's mother and vowing to "make Pablo Escobar feel the effects in his own flesh of his brand of terrorism."[137] Over the next month they

---

[134] Telephone interview, December 3, 1993.

[135] Quoted in Marc Cooper, "Reality Check," *Spin*, November 1993, p. 113.

[136] Andean Commission of Jurists (Lima), "Return of drug terrorism," *Drug Trafficking Update*, No. 34, February 8, 1993, p. 1; "3 Bombs Explode in Colombia Cities," *New York Times*, February 1, 1993; Twig Mowatt, Associated Press, "Bogota bombings kill 4, wound 120," *Washington Times*, February 16, 1993; Douglas Farah, "Bombs Rip Bogota; Cartel Chief Blamed," *Washington Post*, February 16, 1993.

[137] "Colombia Hardens Line In Hunt for Drug Lord," *New York Times*, February 14, 1993; Alma Guillermoprieto, "Exit El Patrón," pp. 72-85.

engaged in numerous acts of terrorism of their own: setting off bombs and fires aimed at other Escobar relatives or their property, murdering a top soccer player from a team allegedly financed by Escobar, destroying, south of Medellín, a five million dollar prize collection of Escobar's antique automobiles, including a Pontiac Escobar believed to have been owned by Al Capone, torturing and murdering Luis Guillermo Londoño White, a businessman linked to Escobar, and murdering defense attorney Raúl Zapata and dumping his bullet-riddled body on a road north of Medellín.[138] After scarcely three weeks in existence, the PEPES had murdered more than forty people.[139]

Following a short six-week truce, the PEPES reemerged in mid-April 1993, when an April 15 car bombing in a posh district of Bogotá allegedly by Escobar's forces killed eleven people and wounded over a hundred. The PEPES abducted and murdered Escobar attorney Guido Parra Montoya and his teenage son Guido Andrés, stuffing the lifeless bodies into the trunk of a stolen taxi. Only after that act did the Colombian government announce a crackdown on the PEPES, offering a reward of one billion pesos (about $1.3 million) for information leading to the identification and arrest of the group's members.[140]

The impunity with which the PEPES operated no doubt contributed to Pablo Escobar's belief that they were a front for the Colombian security

---

[138] Ibid., Reuters, "Escobar foes destroy drug baron's cars," *Miami Herald*, February 18, 1993; Inravisión Cadena 1, "PEPES Group Kills Pablo Escobar Associate," FBIS, March 2, 1993, p. 23.

[139] "Semana de 'pepazos,'" *Semana*, February 23, 1993, pp. 30-33.

[140] Emisoras Caracol, "Kidnaps, Kills Escobar Lawyer," and Radio Cadena Nacional, "Government Offers Reward for Information on PEPES, FBIS, April 19, 1993, p. 32.
Before then, the government seemed almost pleased with the PEPES' audacity. "The PEPES can do what the security forces can't do — blow up someone's house, kidnap people and kill them," said Defense Minister Rafael Pardo. "They are waging a dirty war." James Brooke, "Old Drug Allies Terrorizing Escobar," *New York Times*, March 4, 1993.

forces. Other speculation focused on members of the rival Cali cartel;[141] on friends and relatives of the Medellín cartel's Galeano and Moncada brothers, who were reportedly murdered on Escobar's orders;[142] and finally, on paramilitary leader and former Escobar associate Fidel Castaño, himself linked to several brutal massacres and sentenced *in absentia* to twenty years in prison for the 1988 Urabá murders of over twenty banana workers (see above).[143] Castaño had reportedly fallen out with Escobar over the murders of two Castaño friends, paramilitary leader Henry de Jesús Pérez in 1991, and Fernando Galeano in 1992.[144]

A second group dedicated to Escobar's capture or demise announced its formation in February 1993, claiming to have connections with "people

---

[141] Pablo Escobar's brother Roberto, confined in Itagüí prison, sent Americas Watch seven Federal Express packages denouncing the PEPES, complaining about violations of his rights in prison, and denouncing efforts to murder his brother.

[142] Gerardo and William Moncada and Fernando and Mario Galeano reportedly had cheated Escobar out of a cut of profits from cocaine shipments. Escobar called Geraldo Moncada and Fernando Galeano to account in the Envigado prison, and then ordered their murder. They were kidnapped as they left the prison and their tortured bodies found several days later. The decision to move Escobar from Envigado came after the Moncada/Galeano murders. Ronald J. Ostrow, "Get Escobar Back, Angry U.S. Officials Tell Colombia," *Los Angeles Times*, July 24, 1992; Mary Speck, "Escobar's audacity may be his undoing," *Miami Herald*, February 4, 1993; Mary Speck, "Drug baron faces toughest opponents in ex-associates," *Miami Herald*, March 6, 1993; Inravisión Televisión Cadena 1, "Escobar Seeks Guarantees, Says PEPES Still Operating," FBIS, May 4, 1993, p. 38.

[143] "Quiénes son los Pepes?" *Semana*, March 2, 1993, pp. 22-25.

[144] Ibid.
Henry de Jesús Pérez, leader of the notorious paramilitary group ACDEGAM (Association of Cattlemen and Agricultural Producers of the Middle Magdalena) based in Boyacá, had broken with Escobar in 1991 and had cooperated with the authorities in their efforts to capture him. Pérez had also been convicted, *in absentia*, for the 1988 Urabá murders. Inravisión Televisión Cadena 1, "Former Escobar Associate Castaño Issues Communique," FBIS, April 21, 1993, p. 45; Americas Watch, *Political Murder and Reform in Colombia*, p. 9.

who have been affiliated with security organizations at one time."[145] The group, calling itself Colombia Libre (Free Colombia) said that the "sole objective" of its 150 members was to "combat the terrorism, murders, and tortures perpetrated by Pablo Escobar."[146] The group's leaders said that some of them had worked for the Medellín cartel's Moncada and Galeano brothers, and that current funding came from Colombian industrialists and businessmen. Colombia Libre said that it rejected the PEPES' terrorist methods, seeking instead to penetrate Escobar's organization. In exchange for the cooperation provided to Colombian authorities, the group said it asked the government to target its fight directly at Escobar and not negotiate with him. Leaders of the group said that it would "immediately dissolve" once Escobar surrendered or was killed or captured.[147]

The Colombian government's apparent tolerance of the twin paramilitary efforts aimed at Escobar — some government officials claimed that Colombia Libre and the PEPES were in fact the same group[148] — raised to a new and dangerous level the impunity paramilitary groups have long enjoyed in Colombia. Although the government as well as Colombian citizens may have secretly applauded actions which gave Escobar a taste of his own medicine, an "eye for eye, tooth for tooth"[149] approach to justice only added to the multiplicity of actors responsible for violence in Colombia and invited new cycles of killing. As hideous as Escobar's bombings of civilian targets are, they did not justify the torture and murder of his lawyers and associates, and at times the children of his associates, by paramilitary gangs. As one Colombian official told the *Miami Herald*,

---

[145] *Semana*, Interview with members of Colombia Libre, "Free Colombia Members Describe Group's Mission," FBIS, March 2, 1993, p. 27.

[146] Ibid.

[147] Ibid., pp. 28 and 30.

[148] Mary Speck, "Second group says it's out to nail Escobar," *Miami Herald*, February 17, 1993.

[149] Literally, "three eyes for an eye, three teeth for a tooth," as the PEPES pledged to strike three blows for every bomb set off by Escobar or his associates. "Semana de 'pepazos,'" *Semana*, February 23, 1993, p. 32.

"you can't fight terrorism with terrorism. These groups may start with one objective and then turn into something much more dangerous."[150] With Escobar dead, it is imperative that the government make every effort to identify and prosecute those who participated in paramilitary activity against him.

While Escobar was at large, the Fiscalía intensified efforts to develop evidence against Escobar that would stand up in court, issuing indictments for over a dozen murders including the 1984 assassination of Justice Minister Rodrigo Lara Bonilla, the 1989 murder of leading presidential candidate Luis Carlos Galán, and the 1986 muder of anti-cartel newspaper publisher Guillermo Cano.[151] These prosecutorial efforts are commendable, and against any other Escobar associates identified should continue.

The policy of allowing drug traffickers to turn themselves in in exchange for reduced sentences did not disintegrate completely with Escobar's prison break. Two other notorious kingpins were sentenced in 1992-1993, even if the sentences were grossly disproportionate to the magnitude of their crimes. In December 1992, for example, Cali cartel capo Iván Urdinola Grajales, allegedly responsible for hundreds of brutal murders in the Cauca valley,[152] was sentenced to four years and seven months in prison after confessing to drug trafficking, illegal enrichment, and conspiracy.

Originally sentenced to seventeen years in jail, the sentence was reduced because of Urdinola's confession and the information he provided

---

[150] Mary Speck, "Second group says it's out to nail Escobar".

[151] Douglas Farah, "Colombia's Official Crime Buster," *Washington Post*, February 15, 1993; Alma Guillermoprieto, "Exit El Patrón," p. 75.

[152] Following Urdinola's arrest, U.S. DEA agent Thomas Cash called him "one of the most violent people to be on the face of the Earth...the Cauca River is floating with bodies, including some Colombian national policemen whose extremities were cut off so they cannot be identified." Colombian authorities have also developed evidence linking Urdinola to the 1990 Trujillo massacre (see above). David Lyons, "10 arrested in bust tied to drug lords," *Miami Herald*, April 29, 1992; Ken Dermota, "Colombian police arrest suspected heroin kingpin," *Washington Times*, May 12, 1992.

on other individuals. He was also fined over 750 million pesos, about $1 million.[153] As in the case of Escobar, however, a prison term did not signify the end of Urdinola's activities. In July 1993, Colombian officials discovered that Urdinola was continuing to direct drug trafficking operations from Bogotá's Modelo prison via walkie-talkie communications with members of the Cali cartel living nearby. According to Attorney General Gustavo de Greiff, "nothing" could be done to stop the smuggling of communications equipment into the prisons, given the low salaries of prison employees and the fantastic sums with which drug lords could buy them off.[154]

Medellín cartel kingpin Jorge Luis Ochoa, who had turned himself in in January 1991, also received a reduced sentence after admitting to drug trafficking, illegal enrichment, and conspiracy. Ochoa was sentenced in mid-June 1993 to eight years in prison, of which nearly two and a half had already been served.[155] Ochoa is considered by U.S. officials to be part of the dangerous group of "Extraditables," drug lords who waged a terrorist war of bombings, assassinations, and kidnappings to prevent their extradition to the United States.[156] Extradition was ultimately banned in Colombia's 1991 Constitution. Ochoa also reportedly helped found paramilitary gangs in the 1980s.[157]

Seemingly impressed by the intensity of the violence associated with the pursuit of Pablo Escobar, lawyers for the Cali cartel approached governmental officials in early May to discuss a mass surrender of cartel

---

[153] Inravisión Televisión Cadena 1, "Confessed Drug Trafficker Receives Reduced Sentence," FBIS, December 23, 1992, pp. 30-31.

[154] Douglas Farah, "To Colombian Drug Lords, There's No Place Like Prison," *Washington Post*, September 26, 1993.

[155] "Ocho años de prisión a Jorge Luis Ochoa," *El Tiempo*, June 16, 1993.

[156] The United States waged a long battle for Ochoa's extradition to the U.S., for his alleged involvement in the murder of Drug Enforcement Agency (DEA) agent Barry Seal.

[157] Mary Speck, "Drug lord awaiting sentence," *Miami Herald*, May 30, 1993.

leaders and an exit from drug trafficking.[158] According to reports in *El Tiempo*, however, the traffickers offered to surrender but not to confess their crimes or testify against others in the drug trade. Attorney General Gustavo de Greiff rejected the offer in late October.[159]

The meager results in Colombia's drug war also reflect the pervasive power of money to corrupt those officials ostensibly fighting on its front lines. In late September 1993, the Procuraduría's Delegate for the Judicial Police, Guillermo Villa Alzate, was fired after evidence surfaced that he was in direct contact with Miguel Rodríguez Orejuela, one of the principal leaders of the Cali cartel.[160] According to press accounts, members of the police unit DIJIN based in Cali doctored a police report on the Cali cartel's money-laundering operations, removing the names of the Rodríguez Orejuela brothers. The police report was also leaked to cartel leaders.

Another corruption case compromising officials based in Cali involved the escape from prison of cartel chief and retired army captain Jorge Eduardo Rojas Cruz, about to be charged with murder. Rojas Cruz escaped in June 1993 when he switched places with another man smuggled into the jail with the help of prison guards. Even though Rojas Cruz is white and

---

[158] According to a senior Colombian official, in May the government sent a combined army and police unit to Cali to search for cartel leaders. "There were a lot of people who said, 'Come on, do you really want another Medellín?' But...truly speaking, I don't think we have a choice. Cali has to be dismantled, and even if it wants a surrender, that can't be done without pressure." Michael Stott, Reuters, "Colombia hints Cali cartel may give up," *Washington Times*, June 28, 1993.

[159] "Conditional surrender by traffickers rejected," *Miami Herald*, October 24, 1993.

[160] In late September, a Colombian prosecutor issued an arrest warrant for Miguel Rodríguez Orejuela for his alleged role in a shipment of a ton of cocaine to the United States in 1991. Reuters, "Colombia fires top drug aide," *Miami Herald*, October 1, 1993; Reuters, "Colombian Orders Arrest of Head of a Cocaine Cartel," *New York Times*, September 26, 1993.

his replacement was black, it took the Cali police five days to notify authorities in Bogotá.[161]

Corruption also stymied the fight against Pablo Escobar. Attorney General Gustavo de Greiff stated publicly in March 1993 that pursuit of Escobar had been cut short by "corruption, inefficiency, and cowardice" among members of the *Bloque de Búsqueda*.[162] Six months later, officials of the Procuraduría confirmed that Bloque policemen had alerted Escobar about upcoming operations and had provided him with the license plate numbers, color, and make of vehicles belonging to police intelligence agents conducting surveillance. Official files with the declarations of various informants were also stolen.[163]

With Escobar and his principal associates dead or in custody, the Medellín drug-trafficking cartel has been dismantled. Unfortunately, this has not translated into a reduction in the amount of cocaine reaching international markets. According to the U.S. General Accounting Office (GAO), "the Cali cartel and other trafficking organizations are filling the void left by the Medellín cartel." And the U.S. Drug Enforcement Administration places Cali's share at some eighty percent of the U.S. market.[164]

Indications are that the Cali cartel, once known as less violent and more businesslike than its Medellín counterpart, is stepping up its own violent reprisals against those it considers a threat. U.S. journalist Manuel de Dios Unanue, former editor of the Spanish-language *El Diario-La Prensa*, was murdered in New York in March 1992, allegedly on orders of Cali boss José Santacruz Londoño. The alleged hitman, eighteen-year-

---

[161] Douglas Farah, "To Colombian Drug Lords, There's No Place Like Prison," *Washington Post*, September 26, 1993.

[162] "Se acaba la búsqueda?" *Semana*, September 14, 1993, pp. 38-41.

[163] Ibid.

[164] U.S. General Accounting Office, *The Drug War: Colombia Is Undertaking Antidrug Programs, but Impact is Uncertain*, GAO/NSIAD-93-158, August 1993, p. 22; Douglas Farah and Steve Coll, "Cocaine Dollars Flow Via Unique Network," *Washington Post*, September 19, 1993.

old Alejandro Wilson Mejía Vélez, was arrested in Miami in May 1993. Since Unanue's murder, at least a dozen other people are believed to have been killed in Queens on orders from the drug cartels.[165] The export of violence, coupled with the epidemic of drug-and gang-related murders in U.S. inner cities, establish a macabre bond between the U.S. and Colombian populations, one that shows few signs of being broken in any time to come.

---

[165] Joseph B. Treaster with Steven Lee Myers, "A Dozen Killings Tied to Colombia," *New York Times*, May 16, 1993; Jeff Leen, "Cartel sent teen to silence writer, agents say," *Miami Herald*, May 11, 1993.

PART II

THE MOBILE BRIGADES

Mobile Brigades are the fruit of Colombia's failure to negotiate an end to armed conflict paired with the belief of many powerful elements of Colombian society that despite the military's failure to eliminate guerrilla insurgencies over time, it remains the only institution capable of bringing a definitive end to this decades-old conflict. By the end of the 1980s, some of Colombia's leaders became convinced that peace talks were not working and that the country needed to hone its war-making ability.

This lack of faith in a negotiated end to political violence is reflected in public opinion. A poll conducted by Yankelovich Colombia in May 1992 showed that sixty-one percent of those questioned believed Colombia's armed forces should "take the initiative and utilize all methods to combat the guerrillas."[1] Monsignor Pedro Rubiano Sáenz, president of the Episcopal Conference of the Catholic Church, echoed this sentiment when he told journalists that "(the) government has no other option but to exercise its authority by putting the house in order, with a strong hand."[2]

The centerpiece of army strategy is the Mobile Brigade. The Mobile Brigade is conceived as a highly mobile force equipped with weaponry and vehicles suitable for the country's rugged, often densely forested countryside. While standing brigades are made up primarily of young men serving a twelve-month obligatory term, Mobile Brigades are composed of professional soldiers who volunteer. The number of professional soldiers used in Mobile Brigade operations varies, and can go from 1,200 to 2,000 men.

Mobile Brigades are led by Brigadier Generals who answer directly to army high command in Bogotá, not regional commanders. According to Major General Eddie Pallares Cotes, general undersecretary for the Defense Ministry, this gives them more freedom to pursue highly mobile guerrilla units.

---

[1] "Guerra para rato," *Semana*, June 2, 1992, pp. 30-35.

[2] "El Gobierno debe ejercer su autoridad: la Iglesia," *El Espectador*, November 7, 1992.

"In the past, when a company leader was in hot pursuit of a group of guerrillas, he would have to stop at the departmental border and ask permission of the next commander to cross," noted Maj. Gen. Pallares in an interview with Americas Watch. "Sometimes, because of professional jealousy, the commander would deny permission, thus complicating the hunt."[3]

According to Maj. Gen. Pallares, Mobile Brigade strategy follows a general pattern. The goal is to trap guerrillas, forcing them to flee by a route already covered by troops. The Mobile Brigade begins by "softening up" an area with the bombing of supposed guerrilla settlements and strafing from a variety of aircraft. These preparatory manuevers are carried out by the Colombian Air Force, which often precedes Mobile Brigades in action.[4]

Units of up to one hundred men follow with ground searches (*rastrillos*, literally combing the area). They often carry money with them to buy information and pay for food and inadvertent damages, earning them the nicknames among rural people of *los bolsillones*, big pockets, for the money in the bulging pockets of their fatigue pants, and *carapintadas*, painted faces, for the camouflage paint on their faces. In action they use no identifying rank, unit, or name, ostensibly to protect them from guerrilla reprisals. However, Mobile Brigade soldiers wear distinctive U.S.-style camouflage uniforms.

According to the army, they attack only guerrilla strongholds and are under specific orders to leave the civilian population unharmed. Maj. Gen. Pallares told Americas Watch that Brigade soldiers take special human rights courses that recruits do not and are under specific orders to detain

---

[3] Interview in Bogotá, June 12, 1992.

[4] "Se tecnifica la opción militar," *El Tiempo*, June 7, 1992.

suspects only with the presence of a judge or *inspector de policía*, a civilian who is often the only state authority in small towns.[5]

For Americas Watch, Maj. Gen. Pallares outlined a detailed chain of command and supervision over units engaged in combat. He said that each unit commander must provide his superior with a report of every action, including details of deaths, the destruction of houses, and the number and names of the detained. In the case of a destroyed house, Maj. Gen. Pallares said that the family can initiate an investigation through local authorities, who can identify the responsible commander through normal military channels.

"If abuses beyond the scope of normal combat or orders of the commanding officer are committed, the officer must respond for the actions of his men," Maj. Gen. Pallares told us. "Whenever an action produces deaths, wounded, or detained, the appropriate authorities begin an investigation." A delay in reporting this information is an infraction, Maj. Gen. Pallares added.

A significant amount of Colombia's annual budget as well as new revenue is now dedicated to recruiting, training, and equipping professional soldiers. The 1991 "war tax" went largely to their creation.[6] After the declaration of the "state of internal commotion" in November 1992, Defense Minister Rafael Pardo announced that the government would continue to focus on increasing their number by levying additional taxes.[7]

---

[5] According to Dr. Jorge Orlando Melo, former Presidential Counselor for Human Rights, recruits began taking a twenty-three—hour course in human rights as part of basic training at the end of 1991. The course includes instruction on the Universal Declaration of Human Rights, the Geneva Conventions, and the Colombian Constitution. The version for officers is about double that length. Interview in Bogotá, June 8, 1992.

[6] Defense Minister Rafael Pardo interview in *Nuevo Siglo*, December 7, 1992, FBIS, December 14, 1992, pp. 49-52.

[7] On April 22, 1992, Colombia's Constitutional Court declared unconstitutional Articles 16, 17, and 18 of Law 6, passed in 1992, which obligated all individuals and corporations whose income during fiscal year 1991 was greater than seven million pesos or whose gross assets were greater than thirty million pesos to purchase "war bonds" to increase the capacity of the security forces. The court

By early 1993, the government claimed to have increased the security forces with 8,000 new policemen and 17,000 troops, including 15,000 professional soldiers. The army plans to add 6,000 more professional soldiers in 1993 and now claims a ratio of one professional soldier for every five recruits, up from one in fifty. In addition, the government has invested millions in vehicles, weapons, and uniforms.

There are currently three Mobile Brigades in action: Mobile Brigade 1, based in Granada, Department of Meta, operates primarily in Meta; Mobile Brigade 2, based in Barrancabermeja, Department of Santander, which has seen action in the Middle Magdalena region; and Mobile Brigade 16, based in Yopal, Department of Casanare, charged with defending oil-drilling operations in Arauca and Casanare.[8] In addition there are twenty-one new counterguerrilla battalions attached to some of Colombia's fourteen standing brigades.

This dramatic change in what Colombians call the *pie de fuerza*, number of troops, has already produced a significant increase in the pace and intensity of armed conflict.[9] More troops, vehicles, and weapons than ever before are being used in areas thought to contain guerrilla encampments. During the first ninety days of 1993, the Colombian army reported 320 suspected rebels killed and 603 people, including suspected guerrillas, drug-traffickers, and common criminals, captured, more than

---

characterized the bonds as "a tax disguised as a loan" and ordered the government to repay 220 billion pesos to an estimated 108,000 taxpayers. Subsequently, revisions by the executive in the annual budget have made up much of the shortfall caused by the constitutional ban on "war bonds." Emisoras Caracol, "Constitutional Court Rules War Bonds Unconstitutional," April 23, FBIS, April 27, 1993, p. 30.

[8] Mobile Brigade 1 first saw action in the department of Córdoba against the EPL in 1989. Perhaps the most well-known engagement involving a Mobile Brigade was "Operation Centaur," which began on Dec. 9, 1990, and involved Mobile Brigade 1 and other units in an attempt to destroy the operational headquarters of the FARC, known as *Casa Verde* (The Green House), above La Uribe, Meta. Centaur was part of "Operation Tri-Color," a three-year plan to wipe out guerrillas that ended in 1992. "Sigue operación Caribe en Meta," *El Espectador*, December 23, 1992; and "Brigada 16 para zona petrolera," *El Tiempo*, December 9, 1992.

[9] Interview, CINEP, Bogotá, June 9, 1992.

twice the number recorded for the first three months of 1992.[10] Now, Mobile Brigades and counterinsurgency battalions are involved in most large engagements.

A Pattern of Violations

Despite the government and military's assertions that Mobile Brigades do not commit systematic abuses, some government agencies and independent human rights groups have documented a broad, consistent, and often shocking pattern of serious violations of human rights and the international covenants governing internal armed conflicts. In sharp contrast to army assertions that the Mobile Brigades are better trained to protect the civilian population and are strictly controlled, Americas Watch believes that spreading terror among civilians is an integral part of Brigade strategy and appears to be tolerated and sometimes openly articulated by Brigade commanders.

As disturbing, these tactics have on occasion received the support of the civilian officials charged with investigating and sanctioning abuses. For instance, after concluding an investigation of an incident involving an attack by Mobile Brigade soldiers on a boat used to transport civilians, the Procurador Delegate for the Armed Forces reasoned that such an attack was legitimate since there were guerrillas in the area, even though at the time the shots were fired, guerrillas and civilians could be easily separated.[11]

In this report, we detail extra-judicial executions, "disappearances," rapes, torture, the wanton burning of houses, crops, and food, indiscriminate bombings and aeriel strafings, beatings, and death threats.[12]

---

[10] "Army Reports on Struggle against Guerrillas" from Bogotá Inravision broadcast on April 2, 1993, FBIS, April 6, 1993, p. 29.

[11] See below for the description of this case, which occurred near Achí, Bolívar, on September 29, 1991.

[12] See Appendix One for a list of bombardments by the military that have resulted in civilian casualties.

Mobile Brigades have on repeated occasions failed to distinguish between civilian non-combatants and armed guerrillas, causing avoidable injury and casualty. Frequently, Brigade patrols have forced civilians to walk in front of units to detonate mines or don military uniforms and work as guides. In several cases described in these pages, civilians killed by Brigades have subsequently been dressed in guerrilla uniforms and claimed as combatants killed in action.

This pattern of violations belies the high human rights standards President Gaviria and his ministers claim to uphold. As seriously, it represents an open disregard of Article 3 of the Geneva Conventions, which bind both sides in an internal conflict to respect the neutrality of the civilian population, protect the wounded, detained, and those placed *hors de combat*, and refrain from extra-judicial executions and torture. As in other Americas Watch reports on Colombia, we apply the rules of International Humanitarian Law that are applicable to a "conflict not of an international nature" because those rules provide a meaningful, universal, and non-ideological standard to measure whether an act of war constitutes a breach of the laws of war. We call on all parties to the conflict to abide by these rules regardless of the military or political objectives they pursue.[13]

Rather than endure a Mobile Brigade operation, many rural families abandon their homes. This has created a surge in the number of internal refugees in areas of armed conflict, particularly in the department of Meta and the region known as the Middle Magdalena, both discussed in this report.[14] Those who remain are often forced to join paramilitary organizations that Brigades encourage to attack remaining *"nucleos de subversión,"* subversive centers. Typically, however, the military adopts a broad definition of "the enemy" to include not only armed guerrillas, but also members of the UP, community activists, and local leaders,

---

[13] Later in this report, we also describe violations of these rules by insurgents. For more on the Americas Watch position on Colombia and violations of the laws of war by both sides, see *The Killings in Colombia*, pp. 23-28.

[14] For more on Colombia's internal refugees, see Robin Kirk, *Feeding the Tiger: Colombia's Internal Refugees* (Washington, DC: US Committee for Refugees, August, 1993).

particularly those elected to Community Action Councils (*Juntas de Acción Comunal*), the governing bodies of villages.

Far from encouraging civilians to file complaints about abuses by Mobile Brigades, pursuing perpetrators can be not only difficult but also extremely hazardous to life and limb. Often, victims must struggle to identify the soldiers or units involved, since they wear no identifying rank or name. When local authorities have gone to Mobile Brigade commanders with complaints, they have often been told that the information they seek is unavailable or have simply been lied to. Repeatedly, the victims of Mobile Brigade abuses told us that they were threatened after attempting to make reports or were forced to abandon their homes for fear of being killed. Government investigators have also been threatened and fired upon.

As is clear from Part I of this report, Mobile Brigades are not the only units implicated in human rights abuses in Colombia. However, we believe that Mobile Brigades and the specialized counterinsurgency battalions that work with them have added a dangerous new intensity and level of impunity to human rights violations. Contrary to the assertions of military leaders, Mobile Brigades have not improved Colombia's human rights record, but have seriously eroded it. What some Colombian human rights monitors term "legalized repression" — a phrase used to distinguish government actions from the extra-legal activity carried out by paramilitary groups — is on the rise.[15] Brigades not only reinforce the existing pattern of abuses — including the continued formation and fortification of paramilitary groups — but have pioneered a grisly new attack on Colombia's rural families, particularly those living in isolated areas and most vulnerable to injustice. Like other violations, abuses committed by Colombia's Mobile Brigades enjoy almost total judicial impunity.

The summary of abuses contained in this report is by no means exhaustive. We have left out many reliable reports in the interest of precision and brevity. And human rights groups believe that many violations are never reported, out of fear or a sense of powerlessness. Miles from municipal centers, vulnerable to the next military offensive or paramilitary sweep, many farmers choose to swallow their outrage in the hopes of saving their lives and livelihood. Often, bodies appear in areas

---

[15] Interview, Bogotá, June 9, 1992.

controlled by Mobile Brigades but with no witnesses willing to talk about who might have been responsable for their deaths. One farm family told Americas Watch that during the worst of the fighting, they would simply bury bodies where they fell, since making the trip to the local cemetery was too dangerous.

Hardest hit are peasants who live in areas considered "red zones" because of persistent guerrilla activity. Some say they hide in the hills when they hear helicopters or simply abandon everything and flee. Both soldiers and guerrillas see farms not only as potential targets, but also as sources of food and information. Yet if a peasant is seen giving aid to either side, they risk being identified as an enemy.

A peasant from Meta explains:

> I just work here on my farm, and what can I do if at any moment [combatants] come to my house and ask me to make them breakfast or lunch? I can't deny anyone a bit of food, especially soldiers. If an armed group comes and asks a favor, you can't deny them. I am terrified when they are here, and I must do whatever they ask.[16]

Sometimes, just being near the site of a clash between a Mobile Brigade and guerrillas puts civilians in danger. Such was the case of Helio Valdonado and Herminia Barbosa, a couple travelling with Octavio Bobilla near Arauquita, Arauca, on April 12, 1993. Fired on by a Mobile Brigade patrol, they abandoned their pick-up and ran to a nearby house for shelter. Although witnesses say the three were subsequently detained by soldiers, efforts by the Arauquita mayor, city council president, and *personero* to locate them were in vain. Three days later, peasants discovered their corpses, bearing signs of torture, in an unmarked grave.[17]

Because government investigations are often slow or proceed in secret, in many cases it was impossible for us to verify whether or not an

---

[16] Report of abuse made to the Meta Civic Committee for Human Rights, November 23, 1991.

[17] Memo to Americas Watch from the CAJ-SC and Justicia y Paz, October 1, 1993.

investigation into a reported abuse had been concluded. Where we have been able to follow cases, we have included mention of final decisions and sanctions emitted, if any. However, the mere fact that it is so difficult to ascertain whether or not an investigation has concluded — if, indeed, it took place at all — points to a level of impunity and confusion that can only reinforce the perception among perpetrators that serious abuses will go unpunished.

Mobile Brigade 2 and the Middle Magdalena

The record amassed by the Mobile Brigade in the Middle Magdalena after only three years of operation demonstrates how it has reinforced a climate of terror and injustice in hundreds of rural villages. While this report reviews in greater depth the record of Mobile Brigade 1 in Meta, we include this summary to underscore our assertion that Mobile Brigade abuses are not confined to a single officer, unit, or even Brigade, but are ubiquitous, frequent, and, because they go virtually unpunished, an implicit part of standard procedure.

The Middle Magdalena is named after one of Colombia's principal rivers, which carves a broad valley through the country's center. Made up of parts of seven departments, the Middle Magdalena has long been one of Colombia's most violent regions. Along with the army and police, active there are the FARC, the ELN, and numerous paramilitary groups working with the security forces and drug traffickers.[18]

According to local human rights groups, the Mobile Brigade inaugurated its activities in January 1990. Along with counterguerrilla units attached to the Nueva Granada Battalion, that month the Mobile Brigade carried out indiscriminate bombings and aerial strafing over La Concha, Yondó (Santander), destroying eleven homes and the community

---

[18] For more on the Middle Magdalena, see Carlos Medina Gallego, *Autodefensas, Paramilitares y Narcotráfico en Colombia* (Bogotá: Editorial Documentos Periodísticos, 1990).

building.[19] During the attack, Catalino Guerra, a local farmer, was reported "disappeared" and two other farmers told human rights groups they had been detained, forced to lie in a grave, tortured, and threatened with death.[20] A damage suit brought against the government by La Concha residents has yet to be settled.[21]

That September, the Mobile Brigade again bombed and strafed La Concha along with El Bagre, No Te Pases, and La Poza. This time, soldiers prevented families from fleeing to urban centers, so many took to the hills, surviving on wild fruit. A joint government-NGO commission later documented one murder, one "disappearance," five cases of torture, five arbitrary detentions, and property crimes against twenty people.[22]

The Mobile Brigade was also implicated in five other murders in the area that month, including that of Jacinto Quiroga, a peasant leader and member of a local Christian base community in Bolívar (Santander). According to witnesses, a Brigade patrol had simulated an attack outside his farmhouse. After Quiroga was killed, witnesses said soldiers threatened them, saying Quiroga would not be the only one killed.[23]

A bombardment by Mobile Brigade 2 over Puerto López, El Bagre (Antioquia) on July 19, 1991, resulted in sixty-one civilian injuries

---

[19] Throughout this report, we have identified locations using the following convention: Village, Municipality (Department). According to Colombia's political geography, villages (*veredas* and *inspectorías*) depend on towns, called municipalities, for most public services. Villages vote for municipal mayors and are included in municipal budgets and censuses despite the fact that they are often hours distant by foot. Often, the only authorities in villages are the members of Community Action Councils or *inspectores de policía*, civilians who do preliminary criminal investigations.

[20] Justicia y Paz, *Boletín Informativo*, Vol. 3, No. 1, January-March 1990, pp. 19, 22; and Americas Watch, *The Drug War*, pp. 54-55.

[21] Interview, Pastoral Social, Barrancabermeja, October 19, 1992.

[22] Ibid.

[23] Justicia y Paz, *Boletín Informativo*, Vol. 3, No. 3, July-September, 1990, p. 71.

according to local authorities, although the military later claimed all as guerrillas.[24] Less than two weeks later, the same Brigade was linked to the murder of police inspector and UP member Alonso Lara Martínez and his wife, Luz Marina Villabona, in Sabaneta, Sabana de Torres (Santander). A local farmer later told human rights monitors that she saw how the couple had been forced from a house at gunpoint, bound, tortured for an hour on a railroad track, killed, then photographed with weapons and radio equipment placed by Brigade soldiers near their bodies. Both were presented by the army as "guerrillas killed in action."[25]

Between August and September, 1991, seventeen peasants, including five members of the National Association of Small-holders (ANUC) and one minor, were reported "disappeared" by Mobile Brigade 2 in the Middle Magdalena.[26] Others caught by the Brigade were summarily executed. That was the case of Nain Jaramillo, who ran the communal store in La Alondra, Remedios (Antioquia). Villagers report that he was detained and shot by a Brigade unit on November 22, dressed in a guerrilla uniform, then claimed as a "guerrilla killed in combat." Two weeks later, Bernardo Jaramillo was detained in the nearby village of Gorgona as he accompanied his ailing wife to a medical clinic. Neighbors told human rights groups that he was forced to return to his home, but insisted on reaching the clinic, and was shot as he saddled his horse.[27]

ANUC members were also the targets of Mobile Brigade 2 threats in San Vicente de Chucurí, Santander. After a commission of municipal authorities and ANUC members complained about collaboration between the Brigade and paramilitaries during an operation in La Punta on July 25,

---

[24] Justicia y Paz, *Boletín Informativo*, Vol. 4, No. 3, July-September, 1991, p. 43.

[25] Memo to Americas Watch, CAJ-SC, October 1992; Justicia y Paz, *Boletín Informativo*, Vol. 4, No. 3, July-September, 1991, p. 19; and Denuncia from the Sabana de Torres *personero* to the Procuraduría, August 25, 1991.

[26] Justicia y Paz, *Boletín Informativo*, Vol. 4, No. 3, July-September, 1991, p. 19.

[27] Memo to Americas Watch, CAJ-SC, October, 1992.

1992, Brigade soldiers reportedly threatened ANUC members as "guerrillas... who will be killed."[28]

The Procuraduría Office of Special Investigations was flooded with complaints about Mobile Brigade 2 in 1992, particularly from Antioquia.[29] Often, people were not detained during operations but at roadblocks soldiers set up to limit traffic in surrounded areas. There, documents are checked, packages searched, and food and medical supplies sometimes seized as suspected guerrilla provisions. On October 24, 1992, Alonso de Jesús Luján was detained by soldiers from Mobile Brigade 2 near Segovia (Antioquia) for not having his military service card (*libreta militar*). In both the Zaragoza and El Bagre military bases, he says he was beaten, tortured, and threatened with being thrown out of an air-borne helicopter. For approximately eight hours, he was kept blindfolded and bound in a grave by members of the B-2 (military intelligence). Finally, he was taken out to the woods by men who stabbed him and left him for dead.[30]

Local leaders, union members, and community activists run special risks during Mobile Brigade operations, especially if they belong to the UP. Often, they are singled out as guerrilla sympathizers, harassed, or worse. In October 1992 municipal leaders in Sabana de Torres, Santander, wrote the Procuraduría to complain that Mobile Brigade 2 soldiers had for the past two months burst into events sponsored by the municipality, like flea markets and dances. There, they carried out searches and arbitrary arrests, creating "panic and anxiety" among the population. When the *personero* complained about abuses against the civilian population, he told municipal authorities he was ridiculed by soldiers:

> ... they said to him, well, who was he, what made him want to be the Savior of delinquents! Because every time [the soldiers] detain

---

[28] Letter to Americas Watch from Justicia y Paz, September 13, 1993.

[29] Interview, Procuraduría Office of Special Investigations, Bogotá, March 2, 1993.

[30] Justicia y Paz, *Boletín Informativo*, Vol. 5, No. 4, October-December, 1992, pp. 128-129.

someone he stopped by right away to make inquiries and screw around.[31]

In September 1993, Tirso Vélez, the UP mayor of Tibú, Norte de Santander, was charged with terrorism after Brigadier General Agustín Ardila Uribe, commander of Mobile Brigade 2, publicly accused him of sympathies for the guerrillas because of a poem Vélez published calling for an end to violence.[32] The verse, called "A Dream of Peace," "[constitutes] apology for terrorism... and encourages meetings with guerrillas and collaboration," the general charged.

Torture is a common theme in interrogations carried out by Mobile Brigade 2 soldiers, often occurring in the homes of those detained for questioning and in front of family members, constituting a kind of group torment. In May 1993 Justicia y Paz received reports that Brigade soldiers tortured José Olides Rincón and his brother-in-law, Jesús Gabriel Pinzón, in Rincón's home in Potrero Grande, San Calixto (Norte de Santander) on May 11, 1993. After hitting them, Rincón told the Ocaña *personero* that soldiers hung them from their wrists tied behind their backs with electrical wire and beat them with poles. They used electric current to shock them as they stood in water. While Rincón's mother was forced to play recorded music for some soldiers to dance, other soldiers forced the victims' heads under water for near-drownings. In his statement, Rincón said soldiers ignored his protests that he knew nothing of guerrilla activity in the area:

I told them to kill me, that I was innocent, that I knew nothing of these people they asked me about, much less where the guerrillas were. They answered me that all the peasants said the same thing, that they were innocent, and that (the soldiers) knew that we were all guerrillas. A little later, they pulled down my pants and underwear, tied my testicles with a cord, and jerked it hard... Later, the soldiers let me go

---

[31] Letter to Procuraduría from Sabana de Torres City Council, October 31, 1992; and Letter to the Project Counseling Service for Latin American Refugees from the Sabana de Torres Regional Committee for Human Rights, October 14, 1992.

[32] "A Dream of Peace" appears at the beginning of this report.

after threatening that they would finish off the last seed of my family if I reported them.[33]

Rincón's brother, who lived nearby, also reported being tortured.

Mobile Brigade 2 has also been used to quell legal dissent. In Segovia, Antioquia, for instance, Mobile Brigade 2 detained approximately 240 people on September 14, 1993, to "prevent a disturbance" after a civic strike was called to protest poor road access and a worsening human rights situation. According to reports, soldiers kept detainees overnight with no shelter from a downpour. Members of the Colombian Red Cross and Segovia Human Rights Committee who attempted to provide assistance were denied access. Although they were later released, two community leaders who helped organize the strike were later arrested and held for two days.[34] This constitutes not only arbitrary arrest but also a violation of international humanitarian law, which stipulates that non-combatants be treated humanely and those who liberty has been restricted be allowed to receive relief aid.

Some men are forced to don military clothing and act as guides. The very nature of the Mobile Brigade — dropped into a remote part of the country at a moment's notice — means that often soldiers have very little knowledge of the terrain and so depend on local farmers to guide them. Although sometimes guides work voluntarily, in other instances, peasants have been forced and obliged later to sign statements declaring that service was voluntary. When Pedro Paternina Argumedo was taken off a public bus at a Mobile Brigade 2 roadblock on August 21, 1991, near La Porcelana, Cáceres (Antioquia), he was forced to put on a camouflage uniform and patrol with Lieutenant César Maldonado and Second Lieutenant Reyes for eight days. During that time, he was unable to contact his family. He later testified to the Regional Procuraduría that he suffered "moral and psychological damages to me and my family, for being forced

---

[33] Statement by José Olides Rincón Guillen to Sergio Jacome, Ocaña *personero*, May 13, 1993.

[34] Corporación Colectivo de Abogados "José Alvear Restrepo," *Acción Urgente*, September 17, 1993; and Amnesty International Urgent Action 334/93, September 21, 1993.

from them and because I am responsible for maintaining my two children and wife, who were left abandoned."[35]

Others have been detained when Brigade soldiers arrive with lists of names of supposed "guerrilla collaborators." Such was the case of Ramón Villegas, Wilson Quintero, Luis Alfonso Ascanio, and Gustavo Coronel, detained in San José del Tarra, Hacarí (Norte de Santander) by Mobile Brigade 2 on January 12, 1993. Their detention was later denied by military authorities. Communities in this area reported many abuses committed by Mobile Brigade 2 in January, including threats, arbitrary detentions, "disappearances," and rapes.

Within days, Mobile Brigade 2 delivered the bodies of a number of men who they claimed were "killed in combat" to the regional district attorney's office. Three days later, a unit from the Office of Special Investigations of the Procuraduría and family members were able to identify three of the bodies as Gustavo Coronel, Luis Alfonso Ascanio, and Wilson Quintero.

Fifteen-year-old Luis Ernesto Ascanio, not related to Luis Alfonso, had not been seen since January 26, 1993, when he reportedly left his place of work to return home after becoming concerned about the safety of his family, being held by Mobile Brigade 2. According to Justicia y Paz, his father had been accused by Brigade soldiers of "sympathizing with guerrillas" after being stopped at a checkpoint and found with a copy of *Vanguardia Liberal*, the local newspaper. Subsequently, Brigade soldiers occupied the Ascanio farm. Luis Ernesto's detention was denied by the military.

After a request by the Ascanio family, officials from the Office of Special Investigations of the Procuraduría in coordination with the Military Penal Court oversaw the exhumation of fifteen bodies from the central cemetery in Ocaña, Norte de Santander, on May 21 and 22, 1993. Relatives were able to identify Luis Ernesto's body, which had been

---

[35] Letter from Paternina to Iván Velásquez Gómez, Antioquia Departmental Procurador, Sept. 10, 1991.

dressed in military fatigues. Another body exhumed was believed to be that of Ramón Villegas.[36]

At special risk are women, the elderly, the very young, and school-age children, who are often thought to have information on guerrilla movements. Often, peasants say, children are immediately separated from their parents and submitted to intense interrogation.[37] This is a shocking violation of the provision in Article 3 that persons taking no active part in hostilities be treated humanely, since both children and the parents forced to witness their torture suffer. For instance, Edgar Villamizar, a nine-year-old from El Monhan, Suratá (Santander), was detained with his family by Mobile Brigade 2 on May 7, 1991. While his family was interrogated in the patio of their home, soldiers put a machine gun to Edgar's neck and kicked him until he urinated blood.[38] The following November, a schoolteacher and two elementary school students from Gorgona, Remedios (Antioquia) were brutally interrogated by Brigade soldiers. The children reported being near-drowned in a stream as soldiers demanded information on guerrilla movements.[39]

Women are also seen as sources of information as well as objects of sexual gratification. On May 20, 1992, María Cecilia Sepúlveda reported being forced to take off her clothes, then tortured and detained with soldiers from Mobile Brigade 2 in a boat for a night near San Lorenzo (Bolívar).[40] On November 7, Sonebia Pinzón Herrera and her two-year-old daughter, Marcela, both reported being raped in their home by three soldiers from Mobile Brigade 2, who entered saying that they were looking

---

[36] Memo to Americas Watch from Justicia y Paz, October 1, 1993; Amnesty International Urgent Action 22/93, January 29, 1993; and follow-ups on February 2, February 22, and July, 1993; and Justicia y Paz, *Boletín Informativo*, Vol. 6, No. 1, January-March, 1993, p. 30.

[37] Memo to Americas Watch, CAJ-SC, October, 1992.

[38] Justicia y Paz, *Boletín Informativo*, Vol. 4, No. 2, April-June, 1991, p. 76.

[39] Memo to Americas Watch, CAJ-SC, October, 1992.

[40] CREDHOS, "S.O.S. Población Civil," June 3, 1992.

for weapons.[41] According to Amnesty International, medical examinations confirmed the allegations of rape.[42] Less than a month later, Mobile Brigade 2 soldiers occupied the farm of Nazario Paguena, accusing him of collaborating with guerrillas since a guerrilla unit had camped on the farm earlier in the month. Although Paguena says he explained to the soldiers that he could do nothing to prevent the guerrillas from remaining, he, his wife, daughter, and three-month-old grandson were beaten and threatened with death, constituting not only torture and an attack on non-combatants but a violation of the Article 3 ban on collective punishment. Paguena later told CREDHOS that his fifteen-year-old daughter was raped.[43] In February 1993 community leaders from Tibú and El Tarra (Norte de Santander) reported to the Procuraduría that Mobile Brigade 2 soldiers had raped a woman and a fifteen-year-old girl.[44]

The elderly and very young are often unable to escape the firestorm that accompanies Brigade bombardments and aerial strafing, remaining in their fragile homes where they are prey to attack, cross-fire, and shrapnel. That was the case for Justiniano Rodríguez Sánches, eighty-two, and Teodolinda Agudelo Hernández, eighty, a couple reported killed by professional soldiers in San Lorenzo, San Alberto (Cesar) on March 16, 1991. According to neighbors, soldiers were pursuing a guerrilla when they entered the village to question residents. In the afternoon, the army

---

[41] Justicia y Paz, *Boletín Informativo*, Vol. 5, No. 4, October-December, 1992, pp. 129-130.

[42] The Presidential Counselor for Human Rights was later informed by the Defense Minister that four soldiers from Counter-guerrilla Battalion No. 18 "Cimarrones" attached to Mobile Brigade 2 are in military detention, charged with violent sexual assault, abusive sexual assault against a defenseless individual, rape, and conspiracy to commit a crime ("*acceso carnal violento, acceso carnal abusivo con incapacidad para resistir, violación ... y concierto para delinquir*"). They were to be transferred to the civilian prison in Barrancabermeja.

[43] CREDHOS, *Revista*, January, 1993, p. 8.

[44] Amnesty International Urgent Action 407/92, December 22 and May 10, 1993; and Justicia y Paz, *Boletín Informativo*, Vol. 6, No. 1, January-March, 1993, p. 80.

evacuated three bodies, including the elderly couple. Witnesses say they saw powder burns on them, as if they had been executed. Campo Elías Rodríguez Agudelo, their son, reported their deaths to the local *personero*, asking for an investigation. Later, the army claimed in a press release that the couple were "guerrillas killed in action." Although Rodríguez pressed for an investigation, a year later no verdict had been made. Rodríguez later died and it is not clear what progess has been made on the case.[45] According to CREDHOS, the very young often fall sick and die during the peasant "exoduses" that take place after particularly intense operations, victims of disease and malnutrition.[46]

In other instances, it is clear that soldiers, in search of guerrillas, have failed to try and minimize civilian casualties as required by international humanitarian law, and in fact have acted with a flagrant disregard for the lives of innocents. Such was the case in a noon attack on a farm owned by the Conde family near La Dorada, San Martín (Cesar) on January 6, 1993. Eleven family members, including six minors, gathered to celebrate a birthday were apparently fired upon without warning by a Mobile Brigade 2 patrol. Despite the family's attempt to flee, the attack continued, leaving four children and one adult wounded. According to the farm's owner, Carmen Conde, after the shooting stopped, one of the soldiers told her to give her son water "so that he finishes dying quicker (*para que se acabe de morir más rápido.*)"[47]

In another disturbing incident, Mobile Brigade 2 has been accused of setting fire to a pool of oil created when the ELN bombed the Caño Limón-Coveñas pipeline near the village of Martaná, Remedios (Antioquia). Although the army blamed the ELN for the blaze that consumed several houses, killing ten people, including two children and an eighty-year-old woman, later information and the death-bed testimony of one of the victims

---

[45] Memo to Americas Watch, CAJ-SC, October, 1992.

[46] A exodus is the organized flight of peasants from political violence on their farms. While some families are able to return within days after receiving guarantees for their safety from government officials, others become internal refugees. Interview with CREDHOS members, Barrancabermeja, October, 1992.

[47] Letter to Americas Watch, Justicia y Paz, September 13, 1993.

suggests that Brigade soldiers may have lit the pool on purpose, to implicate guerrillas and punish the village for its perceived sympathies for them. One area resident said a Brigade lieutenant told them, "This is what you get for collaborating with the guerrillas."[48] This incident demands further investigation, to determine whether or not these allegations have merit.

One of the casualties of the upswing in armed conflict in the Middle Magdalena was the Peasant Albergue, a shelter formed in September 1988. Peasants fleeing army bombardments in Santander asked area humanitarian groups, including the church, to help set up a temporary shelter in Barrancabermeja until families could return and rebuild or find more permanent lodging. It remains the only public shelter for internal refugees in Colombia. By 1992, an estimated 2,000 peasants had stayed temporarily within its walls.

But soon after opening, Albergue organizers say they began receiving death threats from the paramilitary group known as MAS (*Muerte a Secuestradores*, or Death to Kidnappers). Adherents are also known as *masetos*. Local human rights groups believe that the MAS maintains close relationships with local police and military commanders, a connection that official investigations in the past have clearly established.

On March 4, 1992, armed men entered the Albergue and kept its guests at gunpoint for several hours. Two months later, Elvia María Córdoba asked for refuge, claiming she had been threatened by the *masetos*. After several days in the Albergue, however, Córdoba confessed to workers that the *masetos* had sent her to the Albergue to collect information. She told them she believed the *masetos* planned to set off a bomb inside. Two days after leaving the Albergue, Córdoba's body was found in a garbage dump outside Barrancabermeja. The Albergue was closed in June 1992 for the safety of workers and guests. An investigation

---

[48] Justicia y Paz, *Boletín Informativo*, Vol. 5, No. 4, October-December, 1992, pp. 123-124; and Mary Speck, "Colombia oil pipeline called tube of misery," *Miami Herald*, January 4, 1992.

into threats on the Albergue continues, but as yet has produced no results. The Albergue was reopened in April 1993.[49]

In 1992 a memo circulated by Mobile Brigade 2 commander Brigadier General Ardila tacitly recognized the army's practice of using paramilitaries and ordered that it be stopped. "It has been very lamentable," he wrote, "for the entire Army to see senior and junior officers paraded before the courts to answer for the results of the operations." Gen. Ardila then ordered his officers "... to prevent units from associating with or employing as intelligence agents, guides, or informants persons who have belonged to guerrilla groups, drug traffickers, private justice groups, or those known to be delinquents."[50]

Americas Watch welcomes this statement by Gen. Ardila in the hope that it contributes to an end in army-paramilitary cooperation. However, we believe it must be followed up with concrete action, including public investigations into abuses and punishment for those responsible. Too often, statements of good will, such as these, have been made meaningless as officers continue to depend on paramilitaries and others to carry out illegal actions, knowing that they face few consequences, if any.

A CASE STUDY — META

Americas Watch has visited the Meta piedmont three times since June of 1992.[51] These rolling hills, where most of the department's population of 500,000 is concentrated, mark the end of the Andes and beginning of the *llanos*, a grassy savannah that stretches into Venezuela.

---

[49] Before it was reopened, Defense Minister Rafael Pardo promised to guarantee the security of the Albergue. Interviews, Bogotá and Barrancabermeja, CINEP, Justicia y Paz, and Albergue workers, June 6 and October 19, 1992; Letter to public officials from Justicia y Paz, October 5, 1992; and Memo to Americas Watch from CAJ-SC and Justicia y Paz, October 1, 1993.

[50] CREDHOS, *Revista*, January, 1993, p. 4.

[51] Americas Watch missions visited Meta in June and October, 1992, and February, 1993.

Like the Middle Magdalena, the Meta piedmont has been the backdrop of political violence for many years. The Mobile Brigade mounted its first full-scale operation in Meta on December 9, 1990. "Operation Centaur," as it was called, was an assault on the General Secretariat of the FARC, located in the rugged Andes above La Uribe. A Mobile Brigade base was later established in La Uribe, where it continues to function.

Isaías*[52] remembers December 9 clearly, because military helicopters appeared over the horizon near his farm in Papamene, about fourteen hours by mule from La Uribe. He says guerrillas passed frequently through the area, but rarely stopped. Like most farmers, he says he provided the water or food they asked for just as he did for passing army patrols. On that day, however, he says Papamene was bombed twice, forcing Isaías and ninety-five others to flee.

By the time they reached La Uribe, they had been joined by 300 more farmers from the villages of Paradera Ukrania and Candelaria, including members of a Páez Indian community. According to the Paeces, out of eleven Páez families, two individuals "disappeared" and a four-year-old child died as they fled the bombardment.[53]

The only aid refugees received upon arrival was from the La Uribe municipality and the ICRC, which provided food and clothing. Isaías was part of a commission that returned to Papamene two months later.

All we found were the skins and bones of my cattle. Later, we reached an agreement with the Mobile Brigade commander so that we could return in March, but by then several of the houses, including mine, had been completely destroyed.

Isaías and other Papamene villagers moved to the village of Esplanación. Hoping to avoid problems with the Mobile Brigade, they say they provided them with a map of the village and a complete census. By then Isaias was the president of the Communal Action Council. But on June

---

[52] Names marked with an asterisk (*) have been changed for security reasons at the request of the interviewee.

[53] Interviews, La Uribe, February 27, 1993.

22, 1991, he says Esplanación was bombed, destroying the school and the documents Papamene villagers had filed with the government for reparations.

Since then, Isaías' family and sixty others have lived as internal refugees. When he has met Brigade soldiers on area trails, he says he has been insulted, hit, and mistreated, and fears being arrested for no cause. Although Isaías lost his cattle and crops, he cannot get loans to restart his farm because he still owes payments on the seeds, fertilizer, and cattle destroyed in the bombardments.[54]

A similar story is told by Lisandra*, from the village of Pata de Gallo. On December 9, she awoke to the sound of bombs landing near her house. When soldiers moved in, she says they seized her cattle for food but did not pay. By the time troops left twenty days later, her house was in ashes and her belongings destroyed. She claims soldiers told her she had no right to complain and shouldn't consider returning.[55]

Since the assault on Casa Verde, the presence of Mobile Brigade 1 in Meta has been constant. Operations are announced by the buzz of helicopters and the slow thud of bombs hitting earth. Farmers say some bombs produce little damage but a lot of noise, terrifying people and animals.

Gustavo*, a member of the Vista Hermosa Communal Action Council, says he tried to work out problems with Mobile Brigade officers. But he says the mere act of asking about detained peasants or trying to get reparations for destroyed homes or animals killed by crossfire put him in danger. He says officers denied abuses and no investigations resulted in action.

Once he says he was detained by Brigade soldiers and tortured:

Sometimes, the army lets no one flee. Because flight means reports on their abuses. So they threaten. They forced me to sign a paper saying I was well treated, even when it wasn't true. Surrounded by twenty or fifty soldiers, what can you do? I was forced to avoid problems... [My

---

[54] Ibid.

[55] Ibid.

wife and I] have had to bury people beside the trail or road, because to go to the cemetery is too dangerous. Where they fall becomes their tomb.[56]

In 1991 he and his family abandoned their fourteen-acre farm without taking clothes or food.

On October 31, a patrol from Mobile Brigade 1 occupied the farm of José Pinto. According to Pinto's wife, soldiers began beating him and threatened him with death. When Pinto's son and a hired laborer approached, they were shot and killed. After the bodies were loaded onto a helicopter, soldiers identified them to their superiors as guerrillas killed in action. As the helicopter lifted off, the area was sprayed with gunfire, endangering the civilians left on the ground. Later that afternoon, several nearby houses were strafed and bombs were dropped.[57]

Over the next five months, three peasants were killed, three "disappeared," and two tortured in Vista Hermosa in incidents tied to Mobile Brigade 1. Frequently, Brigade patrols would stop at farm houses searching for farmers whose names were included on lists of suspected guerrilla sympathizers, threatening the inhabitants with death if they failed to give information. Some men and boys say they were forced to don military uniforms and act as guides or told to walk in front of patrols to detonate mines. For instance, sixteen-year-old Jorge Lozano reported that he was told to put on a camouflage uniform and walk in front of a patrol, so that guerrillas would fire first on him. Lozano was released only after a group of women and children tracked the patrol for two days and finally spoke with the commander, who let the boy go.[58]

Nelson* moved to Vista Hermosa with his family of seven in the late 1980s, attracted by the promise of cheap land. Even though he knew the FARC was active in the area, he says the risk was worth it for the chance

---

[56] Interview, Villavicencio, June 13, 1992.

[57] Denuncia made to the Meta Civic Committee for Human Rights, November 23, 1991.

[58] Meta Civic Committee, *Relación de casos: 1991-1992*; and ASCODAS magazine, Vol. No. 1, March, 1993, pp. 17-18.

to build a farm. His house lay near a road frequented by the army, paramilitaries, and guerrillas, and all stopped for water or food.

But paramilitaries believed Nelson's family sympathized with guerrillas, and apparently shared their suspicion with Mobile Brigade 1. In November 1991, a unit from Mobile Brigade 1 arrived at the house while Nelson was in the fields. His wife, three months pregnant, was detained and beaten. Fearing for Nelson's life, she says she told soldiers that she had no husband. When neighbors, questioned separately, contradicted her story, the soldiers returned.

Nelson told Americas Watch what happened next:

> So more came, they took her from the house and put her in another house all by herself. They told her if she wanted to have the baby, she had to tell them where her husband was. Because of this, because they had all our names and had threatened us so many times, we decided to leave. Really, we were forced to give away the farm. Whoever has the money at hand can get it.[59]

With others, Nelson and his family abandoned Vista Hermosa in 1991 in an exodus assisted by the Civic Committee, which provided food and shelter. According to CAJ-SC, about half of Vista Hermosa's residents have been forced out, replaced by families loyal to paramilitaries.

Internal refugees from Vista Hermosa say that paramilitaries have now set up roadside checkpoints outside town equipped with communications radios. They often walk about with machineguns and go freely in and out of the local military barracks.[60] Peasants who once visited the town weekly to buy supplies now make longer treks to other towns, to avoid the Vista Hermosa paramilitaries.[61]

Even the possibility of filing a formal complaint about what happened to his wife makes him afraid, Nelson says.

---

[59] Interview, Villavicencio, June 13, 1992.

[60] Interviews, Bogotá, June 13, and Villavicencio, October 13, 1992.

[61] Interview with Father Jorge Marulanda, Granada, October 22, 1992.

To put an accusation about these events is simply to put my family in danger. The accusation is broadened, it gets to the authorities for investigation. People get so tired of these things. There are thousands of such accusations, and things remain the same.

Residents of Costa Rica, San Juan de Arama, told human rights monitors that when some military commanders got off helicopters on February 27, 1992, and gathered the population, they publicly accused known UP members of aiding guerrillas. Several of these men had previously been threatened by soldiers. Among the soldiers, villagers say they identified two well-known *sicarios* wearing military uniforms, including Jairo *"El Tuerto"* (One-Eye) Torres, who allegedly took part in a 1991 massacre.[62] The *sicarios* reportedly accompanied the soldiers to a nearby settlement, where residents were exhorted not to "harm" upcoming elections by voting for the UP.[63]

Throughout 1992 reports of abuses by Mobile Brigade 1 flooded human rights groups. For example, in a letter written to Meta governor Omar Baquero Soler by the Communal Action Councils of thirteen La Uribe villages, authorities list seven villages that were indiscriminately bombed and strafed; two "disappearances"; two cases of torture; two houses sacked with belongings robbed; and numerous death threats made by soldiers to detainees they believed were guerrilla sympathizers. All occurred in the last two weeks of February 1992.[64]

In a few cases, Mobile Brigade soldiers have paid for damages on the spot. But in the overwhelming majority of cases brought to our attention, an astonishing callousness to human suffering is more common. This is painfully evident in the treatment given to the Ayure family. Operating on May 14, 1992, near the village of Santander, La Uribe, Mobile Brigade soldiers fired on the Ayure house, where two guerrillas had stopped to eat. Although the government claims that eleven-year-old Martha Cecilia was

---

[62] Memo to Americas Watch from CAJ-SC and Justicia y Paz, October 1, 1993.

[63] Meta Civic Committee for Human Rights, Denuncia No. 15, March 9, 1992; and Meta Civic Committee for Human Rights, *Relación de casos 1991-1992.*

[64] Letter to Dr. Omar Armando Baquero Soler, March 2, 1992.

holding a weapon, later testimony from her mother suggests that soldiers opened fire without first attempting to distinguish who was in the house. The military claims guerrillas killed Martha Cecilia, although testimony given by her mother to the Office of Special Investigations of the Procuraduría indicates that after soldiers began firing, the guerrillas fled and were killed outside the house. Martha Cecilia's mother, Matilde, and five-year-old sister, Sandra, were wounded.[65]

While the two wounded Ayures and the body of Martha Cecilia were transferred to the Military Hospital in Bogotá, three other girls — Graciela, thirteen, Yaneth, nine, and grandaughter Ismenia, two — were flown to the 21st Battalion "Vargas" in Granada with Matilde Ayure's permission. For thirteen days, the three remained in military custody. Yet according to their father, Eusebio Ayure, he was detained for two hours by soldiers after returning to his farm and misinformed about his family's fate. When he finally made it to La Uribe to inquire at the Mobile Brigade 1 base, he was told that his family had been flown to Granada "for security reasons."[66] When he finally travelled to Bogotá, he was prevented from visiting his wife and daughter except in the company of a soldier. He was also prevented from returning to his farm for a week, and lost most of the family's belongings and stock:

The army attacked my house with my wife and five daughters, all minors. They attacked and destroyed it, killing one daughter and wounding my wife and a five-year-old daughter. They grabbed them and kidnapped three daughters... I asked Colonel Lombana to deliver to me the daughters who had not been wounded in this episode. For six days, he tricked me by saying he would bring them until finally he insulted me and never brought them. I returned to Bogotá [where his wounded family was hospitalized]. I hired an attorney and filed a claim. My wife was in the hospital for four and a half months. She left

---

[65] Letter to Americas Watch from Dr. Jorge Orlando Melo, former Presidential Counselor for Human Rights, June 12, 1992; and declaration by Matilde Ayure to the Office of Special Investigations of the Procuraduría, May 29, 1993.

[66] Diligencia de queja rendida por el Señor Eusebio Ayure Bolaños, Office of Special Investigations of the Procuraduría, May 28, 1992.

it handicapped [losing a hand]. My daughter is now handicapped [damaged leg]. I had to go up to my farm and work because the army finished off my entire crop. The house was destroyed. They killed my cattle. And to top it off, my dead daughter's body is disappeared, they never gave it back... This is the greatest pain a parent can have... what pains me the most is that my daughter's body has not appeared.[67]

Matilde Ayure claims that soldiers promised to pay for Martha Cecilia's burial in La Uribe, although the military has as yet given no explanation for their failure to return her body. The case has since been shelved by the Procuraduría Delegate for the Armed Forces.[68]

Eighteen-year-old William Blanco was reportedly detained by Mobile Brigade soldiers on May 7, bound by the hands and feet, then tied with a noose around his neck. In front of his family in the village of La Libertad, family members say soldiers pulled Blanco through a thicket of barbed wire, then taunted him by saying "you smell like a corpse, you are a guerrilla."[69] When family members went to the Mobile Brigade 1 base in La Uribe for information on his detention, Colonel Lombana reportedly denied having him and told them to "go ask the guerrillas." Nevertheless, the family later received unofficial word that Blanco had been seen in a cell in the 21st Battalion "Vargas" in bad physical shape and dressed only in underwear.[70]

After La Uribe residents wrote to Mobile Brigade 1 Commander Rafael Hernández López to protest abuses, he is reported to have responded in a

---

[67] Interview, La Uribe, February 28, 1993. See also Acción Urgente, Corporación Colectivo de Abogados "José Alvear Restrepo," June 5, 1992.

[68] Letter from Eusebio Ayure to Dr. César Uribe, Procurador Delegate for the Armed Forces, June 9, 1993; and "Civiles entre el fuego cruzado," *El Espectador*, May 31, 1992.

[69] Letter from the Peasant Commission of La Uribe-Mesetas, June 5, 1992; and *Colombia Reporta*, Revista Semanal No. 28, June 12-19, 1992, p. 6.

[70] *Actualidad Colombiana*, No. 107, May 14-27, 1992, pp. 4-5.

public speech, "If you want blood everywhere, then there will be blood." ("*Si sangre regada quieren, sangre iba haber.*")[71]

Peasants say they are especially nervous when they walk to their fields or go into town for weekly supplies. Men especially run the risk of being arrested as suspected guerrillas. Such was the case for Gustavo Chavarriaga and Aldemar Bermúdez, two village authorities who visited La Uribe in mid-May 1992 to play in a soccer tournament and buy supplies. On May 17, before leaving for their village of Paraíso five hours away, they agreed to add on their mules supplies bought by an area schoolteacher, who accompanied them with his wife and young daughter. Less than a mile from town, the group was stopped at a Mobile Brigade checkpoint known as Versailles.

Soldiers searched the group and their mules. Hours later, the teacher and his family were released. But the two farmers were held incommunicado for twenty-four hours, then flown by helicopter to the prison in Granada. Much later, family members searching for them learned that the Mobile Brigade claimed the pair had been detained in a guerrilla encampment as they guarded a stockpile of boots, food, and medicine. Chavarriaga was accused of giving guerrillas medical aid. He administered the parish-sponsored village pharmacy, an activity authorized by the military.[72]

Less than two weeks earlier, Paraíso villagers say that Bermúdez had been threatened by Mobile Brigade Captain "Camilo." On February 28, Bermúdez' house had been searched and belongings and money stolen. Soldiers left after threatening him and his children.[73] Two days later, the president of the Paraíso Communal Action Council, Arcadio Ríos, was

---

[71] Letter to Omar Armando Baquero Solar from La Uribe Communal Action Councils, March 2, 1992.

[72] Meta Civic Committee for Human Rights, Denuncia No. 17, May 27, 1992; and Amnesty International Urgent Action No. 170/92, May 21, 1992.

[73] Meta Civic Committee for Human Rights, Denuncia No. 15, March 9, 1992.

"disappeared" after a bombardment near the village.[74] A cursory investigation done by the Procurador Delegate for the Armed Forces into the threats against Bermúdez apparently failed to interview him, family members, or neighbors, yet concluded that since the Meta Civic Committee, which forwarded the complaint, was not an eye-witness, the charge lacked proof. The case was shelved.[75]

Bermúdez was later formally charged with homicide for terrorist reasons, rebellion, and sedition. The formal accusation is based on the testimony of two former guerrillas who now work as army guides and informers, one a minor. They claim he participated in a battle in which a soldier was killed. Apart from the irregularities in his arrest, this charge appears unwarranted since the witnesses for the prosecution in no way implicate Bermúdez directly in the attack on the dead soldier, but only claim he was present nearby. Americas Watch believes this case may involve a serious miscarriage of justice for a farmer without the resources to mount an adequate defense in the public order courts and urges that it be reviewed.[76] Both Bermúdez and Chavarriaga remain in custody awaiting trial.[77]

Less than a month later after the arrest of Bermúdez and Chavarriaga, Otoniel Ladino Muñoz was detained at Versailles and kept in a hole for twenty-four hours. His family was not notified of the detention until three days later, when Ladino was taken in a helicopter to the Granada prison.[78]

Similar treatment befell six farmers from Caño Brasil, El Castillo. Detained in a house as they slept by a Mobile Brigade patrol on January

---

[74] Interviews, La Uribe, February 27, 1993; and Amnesty International Urgent Action No. 170/92, May 21, 1992.

[75] Procurador Delegate for the Armed Forces Exp. No. 022.122.513, December 22, 1992.

[76] Letter to Americas Watch from Dr. Reinaldo Villalba Vargas, Corporación Colectivo de Abogados "José Alvear Restrepo," April 19, 1993.

[77] Memo to Americas Watch from CAJ-SC and Justicia y Paz, October 1, 1993.

[78] Interview, La Uribe, February 27, 1993.

23, 1992, the men say they were bound and tied to stakes, where they remained for thirty-two hours. Eventually, only Dubadyer Rodríguez was taken to the 21st Battalion "Vargas" in Granada, although the military denied the detention. After international protests, Rodríguez was released.[79]

When local and government authorities have attempted to investigate reports of Mobile Brigade abuses, they have been threatened. In May 1992, a commission headed by the Procurador Delegate for the Armed Forces was reportedly strafed by an army helicopter as members examined a destroyed village. One bombardment of La Julia, a village near La Uribe, began two days after a July forum on humanitarian law and peace negotiations sponsored by the municipal government and attended by government representatives. About 1,200 people from seven villages were forced to flee, many with only the clothes on their backs.[80]

Army abuses in Meta led Dr. César Uribe, Procurador Delegate for the Armed Forces, to write to Gen. Manuel Alberto Murillo, Commander of the Army, on March 12, 1992. Dr. Uribe cited charges filed by twenty-five people who had travelled to Bogotá to ask the government for protection.[81] Among the charges were that a thirteen-year-old boy had been detained by soldiers from Mobile Brigade 1, forced to strip, then tortured on the soles of his feet to force him to talk.

Most importantly, the population would like to make it clear that they are not asking for a de-militarization of the zone, but, to the contrary, a benevolent attitude on the part of military authorities and the troops,

---

[79] Meta Civic Committee, *Relación de casos: 1991-1992*; and ASCODAS magazine, Vol. No. 1, March, 1993, p. 19.

[80] Meta Civic Committee, Denuncia No. 23, August 10, 1992.

[81] Such official protests are not new. In 1989 local community and union leaders wrote to the Procuraduría to protest the behavior of the 21st Battalion "Vargas," which they said included abuse of authority, robbery, torture, assault, damage to property, and deliberately causing panic in the area. Amnesty International, "Possible Extrajudicial Execution of Six People in El Castillo, Meta," AMR 23/16/90, April 1990.

which is to say that they are now asking that their attitude toward peasants not be so rough, drastic, and indiscriminate, but that they understand the situation in the sense that if a house search or body search is done or if an operation is planned that it all be done within certain parameters because the population, rather than feel protected, is frightened and forced into a state of persecution... peasants have seen the transport of their weekly supplies slowed down. Not only their belongings are destroyed but also stock and hunting animals (cows, sheep) in bombardments and strafings... when the houses are searched, soldiers seize personal identity documents; which is to say, a panic is being generated within the population... The most elemental human rights are ignored.[82]

Despite frequent protests about the activities of Mobile Brigade 1 in Meta, abuses continue. While this report was being edited, Americas Watch received word of the "disappearance" of seventeen-year-old student Ramiro Guzmán Martínez, reportedly seized by Mobile Brigade 1 soldiers on October 23, 1993, at a house in La Cima, El Castillo. Although Guzmán's parents searched for him at the Granada army base, the military denied detaining their son.[83]

Mobile Brigade 1 has also been active outside Meta, where it has been implicated in serious abuses. In 1990 Mobile Brigade 1 was accused of torturing farmer José del Carmen, detained in the middle of the night in his home in San Cristóbal, Barrancabermeja (Santander). The patrol was led by two officials named "Toño" and "Alfredo." Del Carmen said he was forced from the house, beaten, and taken to a nearby field, where he was bound and beaten again. Soldiers forced a rifle muzzle into his mouth, ears, and nose, then forced him to drink filthy water. At dawn, he was loaded with equipment and made to walk. For a day and a night, he was leashed to a tree.

---

[82] "Ejército desconoce derechos humanos en región de La Uribe," *El Espectador*, March 17, 1992.

[83] Amnesty International Urgent Action 392/93, November 5, 1993.

The next morning, Del Carmen says they hung him from the tree by his arms tied behind his back. While he agonized, he was beaten and soldiers slid a machete across his neck, saying they would cut his throat. Then they forced his pants down. As a soldier sharpened a knife, they said they would castrate him unless he told them what they wanted to hear about guerrillas. In the afternoon, Del Carmen was again made to carry equipment, this time to the San Cristóbal hacienda. In the morning, Toño and Alfredo made him undress and stand in a grave they had dug. They reviewed his identity papers, saying that they would "take his ID to the widow." They filled up the grave with dirt until it reached his chest. Then they appeared to fake an argument over who would get to shoot him.

Del Carmen pretended to faint. Soldiers pulled him out and threw water on him. Later, he says one of the soldiers told him: "You've earned your liberty. People tell us everything during these jobs we do. It's clear you owe us nothing." They forced him to sign a paper they wouldn't allow him to read, and said that if he reported the incident, they would return and kill him.

Nevertheless, Del Carmen reported the sixty-six-hour torture session to the Regional Procuraduría's Office in Barrancabermeja. In December 1992 Del Carmen and five other villagers were forced to abandon their homes when paramilitaries told them they would be killed if they refuse to participate in actions.[84]

Another horrendous incident took place on March 20, 1993, near San Vicente del Caguán, Caquetá. Eighteen passengers were travelling by boat from Tres Esquinas to Cartagena del Chaira when a Mobile Brigade 1 patrol reportedly intercepted the boat at Puerto La Reforma and forced a number of the passengers to disembark and strip. Some passengers were then subjected to torture, including near suffocation in river mud. Among those tortured were Heberto Sánchez Tamayo, Diego Miguel Hernández, and Astrid Liliana Rodríguez. An old man and a boy were also reportedly tortured and remain unaccounted for.

According to the testimonies they later gave to the San Vicente *personero*, Sánchez and Hernández also had their arms and knees twisted

---

[84] Summary by Justicia y Paz, undated; and Amnesty International Urgent Action 16/93, January 21, 1993.

and were later hanged by the feet. Rodríguez testified that she was stripped by the major in charge of the operation and handed over to soldiers, who were ordered to rape her. One soldier refused to carry out the order but the others beat her feet with a hammer and forced a bar of soap in her mouth while they crushed and twisted her breasts.

The three were then transferred to the Mountain Battalion No. 36 "Cazadores" in San Vicente del Caguán where Rodríguez was subjected to further torture. According to her testimony, she was locked in a cell where a sergeant from military intelligence forced her to kneel and placed a revolver on her breast while other military personnel aimed weapons at her. The torturers forced her to repeat texts which implicated her in guerrilla activities. These were tape recorded. When Rodríguez failed in the repetitions, she says the sergeant urinated in her mouth.

Medical certificates consistent with the testimonies of ill-treatment were issued by a doctor at a regional hospital. One month later, Rodríguez's breasts were still badly bruised and may require surgery. All three were later released.[85]

A Climate of Violence

The effect of the Mobile Brigade's blatant disregard for the safety of the civilian population in Meta is easily visible in the hundreds of internal refugee families who now live in Villavicencio, forced from their farms because of bombardments and threats. Many live in misery on the banks of the Guatiquta River, where they lack basic services like water and sewage and are prey to frequent flooding.

Thousands of others have fled the department according to the Colombian Association of Social Assistance (ASCODAS), made up of *desplazados*.[86] They fall into three general categories. By far the largest group are peasants from areas considered "red zones," forced to flee bombardments or army offensives paired with the harassment of paramilitaries. In addition anyone identified, willingly or not, with the UP

---

[85] Amnesty International Urgent Action 121/93, April 21, 1993.

[86] ASCODAS, Vol. No. 1, March 1993, p. 8.

or guerrillas can be subjected to "political cleansing" with little hope of protection from the state. The most visible *desplazados* are UP members and town authorities forced to flee under threat of death.

The ICRC has a permanent office in Villavicencio to attend to the emergency needs of civilians harmed by combat and to visit prisons. However, army officers have frequently accused the ICRC of favoring guerrillas and have made access to battle areas difficult.[87]

Fear, another marker of increased political violence, is never far from the surface. When Mobile Brigade operations start, some families flee immediately, spending days in the bush. Afterwards, paramilitary groups often move in, residents say. Paramilitary members and *sicarios*, hired killers, appear to move with ease in Meta after committing massacres and political killings, despite the fact that the department is one of the most militarized in Colombia, with an estimated 35,000 army troops and thousands of police.[88]

After Mobile Brigade operations, paramilitary groups threaten and murder those they perceive as left-wing or sympathetic to guerrillas, human rights groups contend. In some instances, villagers have reported joint army-paramilitary patrols and operations, where people are detained.[89] When the displaced families return to *catear*, or look around — a word that has come to mean check out the possibilities for return — they discover that their farms and houses have been taken over by paramilitary members. This phenomenon is so common that some observers have suggested that it may be part of a deliberate effort to force "suspect" families from areas considered sympathetic to guerrillas, replacing them with others who strongly back the military.[90] While Americas Watch found no evidence

---

[87] Interview, Meta Civic Committee, Villavicencio, June 12, 1992.

[88] Ibid.

[89] Grupo de Trabajo Internacional por los Derechos Humanos, *Décimo Llamado Internacional*, February, 1993, p. 2.

[90] International Council of Voluntary Anencies (ICVA), *Mission to Colombia: April 11-19* (Geneva: ICVA, 1991), p. 24; and Alejandro Valencia, *"Desplazamiento Interno en Colombia,"* paper presented at the Conference of Jurists on the National

linking this practice to an organized plan, we did hear many reports of such intentional displacement, which is tolerated if not openly promoted by military authorities.

Human rights groups consider Victor Carranza to be the main paramilitary leader in Meta. A rancher, emerald dealer, and reputed drug trafficker, Carranza is said to boast of maintaining the largest private army in the country.[91] To combat the UP and its electoral strength, Carranza and his *carranceros* have apparently made alliances with some police and military officers committed to forcing out Colombians deemed left-wing or sympathetic to guerrillas. In April 1992, arrest warrants for twenty-six men linked to his paramilitary organization in the Middle Magdalena region were issued by Colombia's Dirección Nacional de Instrucción Criminal. According to press reports, Carranza has bought land around Puerto Boyacá, where the MAS was first organized, and is attempting to refortify paramilitary groups believed by the Procuraduría to maintain links to the army's Fifth Brigade, which operates in the department of Santander.[92]

Since the arrival of the Mobile Brigade and subsequent intensification of paramilitary activity in Meta, investigating or reporting on human rights in Meta has become extremely hazardous. "It is worse to report incidents than remain silent," an internal refugee named Pabla* told Americas Watch in her Bogotá home. Pabla and her brother, both UP members, say they were forced to leave Meta by paramilitaries in March 1992.[93] In 1992, some members of the Meta Civic Committee for Human Rights, based in

---

and International Protection of Displaced Peoples in America, Instituto Interamericano de Derechos Humanos, San Salvador, May 13-16, 1992, p. 3.

[91] *Political Murder and Reform in Colombia*, p. 16.

[92] Among those named by the authorities as part of Carranza's organization was the mayor of El Carmen, Santander, implicated in the growth of paramilitary groups in the region known as the Chucurí. "Acusan a Carranza de reorganizar grupos paramilitares," *El Espectador*, April 11, 1992. See also *The Paramilitary Strategy Imposed on Colombia's Chucurí Region* (Bogotá: Intercongregational Commission for Justice and Peace, January, 1993); and *Political Murder and Reform in Colombia*, pp. 8-16.

[93] Interview, Bogotá, October 13, 1992.

Villavicencio, also received death threats and were harassed on the street by men they later identified as police intelligence officers. In July, monitors report that Villavicencio was inundated by gunmen bussed in from the Middle Magdalena. According to witnesees, the *sicarios* distributed weapons in the central park and talked openly of the bounty of eight million pesos, about $12,000, offered for killing three prominent members of the UP.[94] Human rights monitors believe certain well-known *sicarios* travel from killing to killing, movements that are never noted down or limited in any way by the military or police in the area, even at checkpoints. In some instances, groups of *sicarios* have been seen leaving the local military barracks scant hours before a killing. Afterwards, they vanish like river mist.[95]

All three UP members threatened by paramilitaries asked for guarantees from the state. Nevertheless, the two bodyguards assigned to Dr. José Rodrigo García, vice-president of the Meta assembly, were suspended on Nov. 25. Two days later, García was murdered in front of his house by a man on a motorcycle, a method used by *sicarios*.[96] Pedro Malagón, the

---

[94] Letter from Meta Civic Committee for Human Rights, undated.

[95] Professional soldiers have also reportedly hired themselves out as *sicarios*. Such was the case involving Wilson Eduardo Daza Rosso and José Alberto Cristiano Riaño, members of a counterguerrilla company belonging to the Revéis Pizarro Battalion in Saravena, Arauca. According to witnesses, they killed *El Tiempo* journalist Henry Rojas Monje on December 28, 1991, for the equivalent of $120.00. They were allegedly paid by the municipality of Arauca, whose mayor, José Gregorio González Cisneros, apparently had a dispute with the journalist over money. They were subsequently arrested by the DAS. "Alcaldía de Arauca tenía en su nómina a sicario que mató a periodista," *Nuevo Siglo*, April 15, 1992.

[96] At the time of his death, García was leading the investigation into the murder of his wife, the former mayor of El Castillo, and four others on June 3 (described in the following pages). Letter to President César Gaviria Trujillo from Americas Watch, December 8, 1992.

UP member who replaced García in the assembly, later reported being followed by men he believes may be *sicarios*.[97]

On April 19, 1993, Delio Vargas Herrera, a Civic Committee member, UP member, and president of the Meta chapter of ASCODAS, was "disappeared." Delio Vargas was last seen in the "20 de Julio" neighborhood of Villavicencio, where he was abducted in front of his wife by five heavily armed men. Vargas, a co-founder of the Meta Civic Committee for Human Rights, had helped organize a forum on peaceful alternatives to political violence, held subsequently on April 23.

The Colombian Presidential Counselor on Human Rights later informed Americas Watch that following an investigation undertaken by the Procuraduría's Office of Special Investigations and the Technical Investigation Unit of Villavicencio, the vehicle used to transport Vargas and its driver, Hernando Moreno Martínez, were identified and Moreno placed under arrest. Moreno is a former army second sergeant and army intelligence informant. He is also reputed to have been a key operative in Víctor Carranza's paramilitary force for the past five years. While Americas Watch welcomes the investigation into Vargas' "disappearance" and the possible participation of Moreno, it must be noted that many such investigations are opened and very few lead to the prosecution and conviction of those actually responsible for the human rights violation. Vargas remains "disappeared."[98]

This climate of fear and suspicion has been especially hard on health professionals, often accused by the security forces of having given medical treatment to guerrillas. This is a direct violation of the provisions in the Geneva Conventions that protect medical personnel from arrest or attack for carrying out their duties regardless of the identities or sympathies of patients.

---

[97] Letter to Manuel Velasco [sic] Clark, staff attorney, the Inter-American Commission for Human Rights, from Aída Abella, President, Patriotic Union, June 28, 1993.

[98] Letter to Americas Watch from Mariana Escobar, office of the Presidential Counselor for Human Rights, June 2, 1993; and Memo to Americas Watch from CAJ-SC and Justicia y Paz, October 1, 1993.

Threats against and attacks on doctors and medical clinics were common in 1992. In September and October, one Meta doctor was "disappeared" and two were murdered:

◆ On September 11, Dr. Armando Rodríguez Parrado, director of the hospital in the municipality of Restrepo, was seized from his work place by five heavily-armed men, who apparently had his name noted down on a piece of paper. Rodríguez remains "disappeared."

◆ Dr. Edgar Roballo Quintero, thirty-seven, director of the hospital in the municipality of San Martín was "disappeared" on October 4 from the hospital. His cadaver was found the next day on the highway between San Martín and Cubarral, his body showing multiple bullet wounds and signs of torture.

◆ Surgeon Alvaro Diego Escribano was shot down by *sicarios* at the Llano Clinic Center in Villavicencio, where he worked, on October 29. Escribano had been receiving death threats for his work with poor residents of the city.[99]

All three worked with the UNUMA health cooperative in Villavicencio, whose name is an indigenous word for unity. UNUMA works with the internally displaced. In October the UNUMA office was practically besieged by threatening telephone calls and the presence of men on motorcycles and cars without license plates, the vehicles of choice for *sicarios* and police intelligence officers. The clinic had to be closed. The remaining staff, including two nurses, two doctors, two bacteriologists, and an economist, were forced to flee the city with their families.[100] When Colombians who have received death threats travel in Meta, they must do so using circuitous routes and remain on the look-out for ambush, even in areas theoretically

---

[99] ASCODAS magazine, Vol. No 1, March 1993, p. 15; and National Coordinating Committee for Human Rights and Victims of the Dirty War (CONADHEGS), *Acción Urgente*, October 29, 1992.

[100] Letter to CINEP from UNUMA, November 27, 1992.

under military control. On June 3, 1992, men reportedly wearing army uniforms ambushed and killed the mayor of El Castillo, the out-going mayor, and three others. Ex-mayor María Mercedes Méndez, newly-elected mayor William Ocampo, Treasurer Rosa Peña, animal husbandry specialist Ernesto Saralde, and driver Pedro Agudelo — all members of the UP — had just delivered to regional authorities in Villavicencio an official complaint about abuses by the armed forces against the civilian population. Municipal worker Wilson Pardo García was wounded, but managed to escape.[101]

Four months later, no judge had been assigned to lead an investigation into the killing according to Eixenover Quintero, the El Castillo *personero*. According to the Defensoría, the case remains in an "initial stage" of investigation (*indagación preliminar*). Quintero himself replaced a UP colleague murdered in circumstances suggesting the work of paramilitaries.

"The state is indifferent," Quintero told Americas Watch. "We don't know in what moment they will strike. Our work as public officials is therefore very limited and we can't travel without taking on a great risk. We live in a state of permanent, daily threat."[102]

Five years earlier, paramilitaries had set an ambush for another El Castillo mayor and UP member in the same spot. Although the mayor did not board the public bus he had planned to that morning, the ambush was carried out as planned, killing seventeen. Known as Caño Cibado, this thickly-forested dip in the road provides excellent cover. According to El Castillo authorities, it is frequently used as a *botadero de cadáveres*, a place where bodies are tossed.[103]

Statistics gathered by the Defensoría show that the department of Meta is second only to the department of Antioquia in terms of the murder of UP members. Of the 717 murders of UP members documented by the Public Defender from 1985 until September 1992, eighteen per cent took place in

---

[101] "El Castillo: matanza de funcionarios," *El Tiempo*, June 4, 1992, p. 2.

[102] Interview with El Castillo authorities, El Castillo, October 22, 1992.

[103] Ibid.

Meta.[104] Although international protests about these killings are essential, local monitors say, they have also contributed to increased risk for those who investigate and report on abuses.[105]

Americas Watch representatives experienced the climate of violence that surrounds Mobile Brigade 1 first-hand during a March 1993 mission to Colombia. Mission members visited the town of La Uribe, where a Mobile Brigade 1 base is located. The mission had been invited by the town council and representatives of some of the forty-five villages that belong to La Uribe municipality. Local authorities have attempted to maintain good relations with Brigade commanders and soldiers despite a wide range of abuses in the countryside. Since an off-duty Brigade soldier killed a civilian with a grenade during a fight outside a discotheque in 1991, soldiers on leave have not been allowed to enter the town at night according to a town council member. However, soldiers do patrol the town at night as part of their regular duty.[106]

Town authorities described relations as improved since the conclusion of a peace forum sponsored by the mayor and held in July 1992. The Brigade commander attended along with government representatives, human rights monitors, and area villagers. Nevertheless, Mayor Saúl Rengifo described the calm as "apparent." In recent months, several La Uribe authorities and peasants had been ambushed and murdered on the way to Villavicencio, an eight-hour journey. To attend to official business, people must travel from La Uribe through Mesetas, considered a paramilitary stronghold. From there, the potholed, rutted dirt road descends to a junction with a paved highway outside Granada, another paramilitary center that is believed to be closely controlled by Carranza.

---

[104] Defensoría del Pueblo, *Estudio del caso de Homicidio de Miembros de la Unión Patriótica y Esperanza, Paz y Libertad: Informe para el Congreso, el Gobierno y el Procurador General de la Nación.* (Santafé de Bogotá: October, 1992), p. 68.

[105] Interview, Villavicencio, June 22, 1992.

[106] The name of the soldier who killed the civilian was never released to town authorities. It is not clear if any action was ever taken to punish him. Interviews, La Uribe, February 27, 1993.

Travellers must then pass through San Martín and Acacias, where Carranza is believed to maintain "schools" for paramilitaries, teaching them surveillance, ambush, and other techniques.[107] Until reaching Villavicencio two hours later, UP members, community activists, and human rights monitors are prey to ambush or being pulled off the road and summarily executed.

For example, on September 14, 1991, Carlos Julián Vélez, his wife, eight-year-old son, and brother were murdered on the outskirts of Mesetas by heavily armed men. Vélez, a deputy to the departmental assembly and UP member, had recently denounced the presence of *sicarios* in the area who he believed were waging an extermination campaign against UP members.[108]

Jorge Enrique Delgado, a UP member, was the Mesetas treasurer until he resigned in October 1992 after repeated threats on his life. He became Mesetas treasurer after his predecessor was murdered after assuming the post from another murdered colleague. Along with other human rights monitors, Delgado has identified individual paramilitaries who work in Meta, known by their nicknames: Piglet, Paraffin, Bull Frog, Black Shirt, and Gunpowder.[109]

As a municipal official, I have submitted twenty-nine declarations of witnesses to paramilitary activity and links with the security forces, but not one has resulted in serious action. Everyone in Mesetas knows who the paramilitaries are, and who they work with. But is action ever taken against them? To the contrary, these killers are considered allies of the police and military.[110]

---

[107] Interview, Justicia y Paz, Bogotá, March 1, 1993.

[108] According to the Public Defender's office, the investigation into this quadruple homicide has so far produced an arrest warrant for one suspect and the detention of a second. *Political Murder and Reform in Colombia*, pp. 5-6; see also ASCODAS magazine, Vol. No. 1, March, 1993, p. 12.

[109] Lechona, Parafina, Sapotoreado, Camisa Negra, Grano de Pólvora.

[110] Interview, Villavicencio, October 22, 1993.

The man who replaced Delgado, Julio Serrano Patiño, was fired on in his car in Mesetas by a number of armed men in another vehicle on April 16, 1993. Following the attack, he was forced into his assailants' vehicle and driven to an unknown destination. Serrano's driver managed to escape although he was injured in the attack. Serrano remains "disappeared."[111]

The apparent calm in La Uribe vanished the morning of the mission's departure, when La Uribe awoke to paramilitary-style death threats spray-painted in red on three buildings. The threats were in the form of a question mark followed by a Christian cross: (?+). Residents interpreted the message thus: "Who will be the next to be murdered?" Hand-delivered death threats had been slipped under the doors of two town council members, the president of the Communal Action Council and a store owner. Since only Brigade soldiers are about at night, suspicion rested on them. Americas Watch is aware of no investigation into the incident, even though it was inmediately denounced to the Defense Ministry. The threats appeared to be a direct result of the Americas Watch mission.

Impunity

For the most part, military authorities deny abuses by Mobile Brigades are commonplace or link reports to an alleged defamation campaign sponsored by guerrillas against the government.[112] For instance, when

---

[111] Amnesty International Urgent Action 127/93, April 23, 1993.

[112] Such a defense is not unique to Mobile Brigades or specialized counterguerrilla units. After intense operations by the 2nd Brigade against guerrillas in the Sierra de Perijá, Cesar, in June and July, 1990, Brigadier General Juan Salcedo Lora told reporters that the reports of abuses, torture, murder, and the mass exodus of peasants from thirteen villages was "an action organized by FARC sympathizers and political organizations allied to this movement and the self-defense groups that have been previously organized by them. In this way they produce a movement meant to impede the continuation of military operations against their camps or against FARC columns." Nevertheless, area authorities, including elected congressional deputies, mayors, and ICRC representatives collected hundreds of testimonies documenting widespread abuses. Letter to Ismael Alonso Martínez Charry, Cesar Regional Procurador, from Deputy Alexis Hinastroza et al and medical report on the torture of peasant Pablo Muñoz Torrez, June 28; letter to the

residents of Tienda Nueva, Yondó (Antioquia) and San Vicente de Chucurí (Santander) along with CREDHOS denounced to the Procuraduría the murder of Henry Delgado and torture of ANUC leader Gabriel Flórez in September 1990 by members of a Mobile Brigade, Mobile Brigade Commander Hugo Tovar said to the press that CREDHOS "is an organization dedicated to helping subversion." In neither case were those responsible for the abuse punished.[113] Often, military leaders qualify peasants who denounce abuses or flee bombardments *en masse* as pawns in a public relations campaign orchestrated by guerrillas to smear the military.[114]

Human rights monitors, community activists, and journalists come under special fire for reporting abuses. For some, Mobile Brigades are just one more source of threats and harassment, like the police, standing brigades, or paramilitaries. This was the case for Alfonso Palacio, a well-known peasant activist, community leader, and elected official from Río Viejo, Bolívar. The target of frequent harassment and threats since 1985, Palacio says he has recently been receiving death threats from soldiers attached to Mobile Brigade 2. On May 6, 1993, soldiers from the local Nariño de Magangue Battalion illegally searched his house while he was not present, destroying his library. Instead of leaving, the soldiers remained there for several days, saying to his family that Palacios had saved himself this time but that they would soon "fix him." On May 28, while Palacio was with an official commission riding on a public bus, soldiers boarded the vehicle and sat next to him, pausing long enough to say "this one smells like a coffin (*huele a cajón*)."[115]

Personeros in several towns where Mobile Brigades are active have told Americas Watch that their work is made virtually impossible by the

---

ICRC by Víctor Ochoa Amaya, mayor of Becerril, on July 2; and "No hay bombardeo contra campesinos," *El Heraldo*, July 3, 1990.

[113] CAJ-SC, "*Panorama de los Derechos Humanos en Colombia: 1990*," December 4, 1990, p. 2.

[114] "Cada diez horas muere un guerrillero," *El Tiempo*, June 29, 1992.

[115] CINEP, Acción Urgente Internacional, June 8, 1993; and Amnesty International Urgent Action 187/93, June 11, 1993.

atmosphere of threat and fear fostered by the Mobile Brigade. This *personero* asked for anonymity:

It is difficult, almost impossible to do my job in a war zone. First, I must defend myself. The soldiers call me a guerrilla, a communist, to my face. To me, it is clear that the armed forces are allowed a special kind of conduct. Instead of protecting the civilian population, the Mobile Brigade strikes it. Then, anyone who flees is called a guerrilla supporter.[116]

Another *personero* from the Middle Magdalena made a heartfelt appeal to the Procaduría after processing a number of charges against Mobile Brigade 2, with no subsequent efforts by government officials to investigate, prosecute, or punish:

It is a shame that that those who by constitutional and legal mandate are charged with defending life, honor, and the belongings of our people are the first to ignore such principles... *Personeros...* must either report or shut up, and if we do the former we could be called either army informants or guerrillas depending on the case, and if we shut up we could be investigated for failing to do our duty. In the middle of this public disorder, we all need the national government to guarantee minimum human rights at least in terms of their responsibilities and determine who is at fault.[117]

Despite these obstacles, human rights groups and government investigative agencies have gathered enough information on the methods and record of Mobile Brigades to outline not only a pattern of abuse, but also of impunity. Americas Watch is aware of several important investigations of alleged abuses by Mobile Brigades carried out by the

---

[116] Interview. Name and date withheld by request.

[117] Memo to Americas Watch from CAJ-SC, October 1992.

Office of Special Investigations of the Procuraduría.[118] Repeatedly, credible evidence has been found linking Mobile Brigades to serious abuses. However, when cases are passed to the Procurador Delegate for the Armed Forces for action, they are often seriously delayed, shelved, or result in the acquittal of the military officers involved. Often, decisions are based on only the most cursory of investigations, which fail to take into account the testimony of victims or eyewitnesses. When such testimony is included, it is frequently disregarded and no explanation given. Rather than provide a "bulwark of democracy," as Procurador Delegate Dr. César Uribe has asserted, a procedure that leaves accountability in the hands of the military perpetuates unilateral force and reinforces the patterns of abuse that make any real exercise of democracy impossible.

For instance, the Office of Special Investigations concluded that there was merit to accusations made against Mobile Brigade 1 involving the "disappearance" and torture of Jorge Palomino and "disappearance" of Rodrigo Giraldo on April 22, 1992. The Office found that both had indeed been detained, a fact registered in the Brigade's daily operations record. However, only after Palomino managed to escape from military custody did the Brigade cease denying having detained the pair.

According to one witness interviewed by the Procuraduría who claimed to have spoken with Palomino after his escape, Palomino had been severely tortured:

...(he said) that they had filled his mouth with mud and then they threw water on him and covered his nose and forced him face down on the ground and then stuffed a rag down his throat and one of them got on top of him saying he would make him sing, and when they saw that he was just about to die, finally they released him.

Nevertheless, the Procurador Delegate delayed eight months after receiving the case from the Office to conclude that since Palomino had managed to escape, his detention "is not demonstrated." No mention was made of the allegation of torture or the unacknowledged detention of Giraldo. In addition the Procurator Delegate asserts that since the Meta

---

[118] Interview, Bogotá, March 2, 1993.

Civic Committee, which had forwarded the original complaint, had no direct knowledge of the abuse, the detentions "are not demonstrated."[119]

Americas Watch believes that in this case, as in many others that have come to our attention, the response of the Procurador Delegate has been seriously deficient. It fails to meet the criteria we have elaborated in our many reports on Colombia for fair and impartial inquiries into reports of abuse by the security forces. Evidence forwarded by the Office of Special Investigations was ignored, and no effort was made to supplement it with additional testimony from witnesses. The fact that a prisoner escapes from illegal custody does not erase the abuse of detaining him without proper procedures in the first place.

In a particularly disturbing decision made by the Procurador Delegate for the Armed Forces on December 30, 1992, Colombia's maximum supervisory authority for the security forces openly excused and condoned an act of war that directly violates international humanitarian law, in this case deliberate firing upon civilian non-combatants in a war zone. The case involved the death of two peasants travelling in a public boat (*chalupa*) in September 1991 near Montecristo, Achí (Bolívar).

According to two eyewitnesses interviewed later by the Achí *personero* and the Regional Procurador, the nine passengers and owner boarded early in the morning and embarked on a daily route much like that of a municipal bus. Enroute, two guerrillas hailed the owner, who paused to pick one up.

Georgina Tapias, a passenger who was wounded, recounted what happened next:

> When the guerrilla was boarding... a boat carrying soldiers appeared and the guerrilla asked who they were, so the boat owner told him it was the army and [the guerrilla] got off running and that was when the army began to shoot hot lead at the boat and those of us there... we

---

[119] Conclusions of the Procurador Delegate on reports of abuses by Mobile Brigade 1 in Meta, Exp. No. 022.122.513, December 22, 1992; and Letter to Mauricio Gutiérrez Echeverry, Vice-Procurador General of the Nation, from Justicia y Paz, June 10, 1993.

threw ourselves into the water and the boat sank with the two dead passengers aboard. We screamed that we were not guerrillas, that we were passengers...

Another wounded passenger concurred that soldiers, not guerrillas, initiated firing. Nevertheless, in his investigation, the Procurador Delegate concluded that guerrillas had initiated the attack from surrounding hills, forcing soldiers to "repel the armed attack and then, yes, help the wounded in the encounter." The investigation concluded that the situation of armed confrontation in the area "justified" an attack of this nature, in the interest of "defending community interests."[120]

Americas Watch believes that both guerrillas and the army are to blame for these deaths. Guerrillas should not put the civilian population in danger by riding while uniformed and armed on public transportation in areas of conflict. However, the burden of these deaths, we believe, rests squarely on the army, which has the obligation under international humanitarian law to minimize harm to the civilian population. The legitimate goal objective of capturing a fleeing suspect was far outweighed by the illegitimate fire on non-combatants.

We attempted to meet with Dr. Uribe to discuss these problems in March 1993, but he failed to appear at a scheduled and confirmed appointment.

Most cases involving alleged violations by Mobile Brigades are first heard in military courts where the judge is the unit or brigade commander. Often, this means that the officer who orders an operation and bears responsibility for its execution is put in the position of judging alleged violations by subordinates. As with proceedings against regular soldiers, proceedings against members of professional units are shrouded in secrecy.

---

[120] Letter to the Procurador General from Justicia y Paz, June 6, 1993; and Exp. No. 022 120.332.- from Dr. César Uribe, Procurador Delegate for the Armed Forces, December 30, 1992.

However, we believe that in the majority of cases, either the accused are absolved or the case is shelved for "lack of proof."[121]

Some professional soldiers implicated in abuses have been punished, albeit many years later. For instance, in June 1992 military courts found a captain and two sergeants belonging to the "Falcon" counterguerrilla company guilty of the September 1986 murder of six workers in La Zalazar, Belmira (Antioquia) and sentenced them to sixteen years in prison. According to the evidence presented to the courts, Capt. Tomás Ignacio Monroy Roncancio, First Sergeant Samuel Jesús Mejía González, and Second Sergeant Marco Aurelio Mendoza Mena detained the men as "suspected subversives," forced them into a cave, then one by one slit their throats.

Once a conviction is announced, surviving family members can make a claim for reparations to regional or national authorities. For instance, the family of one of the victims, Angel de Dios Londoño, made such a claim to the Council of State (*Consejo de Estado*), which ordered the state to pay reparations of 5,000 grams of gold, the equivalent of $60,000 dollars. In its decision, the State Council reported that, "Once their work was finished and with their hands still bloody, the sergeant (Mendoza) announced in a calm and serene voice, 'Nothing has happened. This is not the first time...'" The families of the five other victims await a decision.[122]

In January 1993 the Administrative Tribunal in Antioquia ordered the state to pay the equivalent of 1,200 grams of gold ($36,000) to the family of a spokesperson for the EPL, detained by soldiers and then executed on a military base in San Pedro de Urabá in 1985.[123]

But in the few cases where the government has meted out punishment to soldiers convicted of abuses, like the La Zalazar case, sentences are light in comparison to those applicable to civilians convicted of similar crimes. In ordinary courts, for example, the sentence for premeditated homicide is

---

[121] In Spanish, *sobreseimiento definitivo por falta de pruebas*. Asociación SETA, *Misión de Identificación de Derechos Humanos en Colombia* (Brussels, Belgium: Asociación SETA-La Comunidad Europea, May, 1993), p. 59.

[122] "Condenada Nación por muerte de 6 labriegos," *El Tiempo*, June 1, 1992.

[123] "Condena a la Nación por $24 millones," *El Mundo*, January 22, 1993.

twenty-four years. In public order courts, this same crime is subject to a thirty-year sentence.[124]

At the end of 1993, the Defense Minister asked the national Congress for six months of extraordinary powers for the president to restructure the military, particularly in the area of discipline. Based on a document submitted to Congress on September 2, the proposed reforms will apparently focus on the current rules governing the disciplinary system, in particular how claims and punishments are handled. Interviewed in Paris about the proposal, Defense Minister Pardo confirmed that human rights violations "continue in Colombia, which cannot be denied."[125]

Although Americas Watch believes it is premature to comment on a reform proposal that remains vague and undefined, we encourage the Defense Minister's effort to review this system, so clearly deficient. However, if reforms fall short of mandating that soldiers accused of abuses be tried in civilian courts — the only way to guarantee fair and impartial trials — no tinkering with the existing bureaucracy will address the serious faults so evident here.

GUERRILLA ABUSES IN CONFLICT ZONES

Since it began reporting on human rights in Colombia, Americas Watch has called on the guerrillas to cease practices that violate international humanitarian law. Despite the guerrillas' calls on the government to respect human rights and abide by minimum standards of the laws of war, guerrillas themselves commit frequent abuses of those same standards. While at one time we could say that guerrillas in general obeyed certain norms — in particular, in the way they treated members of the security forces taken prisoner — over the past year we have received highly disturbing reports of the killing of these prisoners, often including

---

[124] Telephone conversation with CAJ-SC, November 16, 1993.

[125] "Defense Minister Proposes Military Reforms," *El Espectador*, September 16, FBIS, October 25, 1993, pp. 58-59.

the use of torture.[126] The killing of prisoners is explicitly prohibited by Common Article 3 of the Geneva Conventions, and constitutes an egregious violation of the right to life.

Although we have been unable to confirm independently all of the cases claimed by the government, we have received other reports from reliable sources indicating that such abuses are not uncommon. According to the DAS, for instance, officer Fredy Zamora Sánchez was seized by militants of the CGSB on March 7, 1992, while he travelled on a public bus in the Norte de Santander department. He was forced from the bus and apparently murdered. According to news reports, guerrillas prevented the authorities from retrieving the corpse for three days. An autopsy revealed that Zamora had been beaten and stabbed before being shot twice in the head and once in the neck. His face had been mutilated.[127]

In addition certain guerrilla actions — like attacks on police stations when civilians are present or the bombing of government property near civilian dwellings — do not sufficiently take into account the risk to the non-combatant population and so constitute a violation of the laws of war. Repeatedly, civilians who work in or near such places or simple passers-by have been needlessly injured, maimed, or even killed by tactics guerrillas could easily avoid.

Guerrillas also frequently engage in combat near or in villages and towns, trapping people in furious crossfire. In repeated instances, it has been impossible for investigators afterwards to determine just who caused civilian casualties. For instance, in combat near Apartadó in November 1991, about one hundred people were forced to flee a confrontation between the army and militants belonging to the Fifth Front of the FARC. A three-year-old child was killed and a school destroyed.[128] Americas Watch has also received reports that guerrillas fleeing army pursuit have

---

[126] For additional information on Americas Watch documentation of violations of the laws of war by guerrillas, see *Political Murder and Reform in Colombia*, pp. 60-68; *The Killings in Colombia*, pp. 23-33; *The "Drug War" in Colombia*, pp. 64-71; and *Human Rights in Colombia As President Barco Begins*, pp. 44-47.

[127] "Yo también acuso," *Semana*, December 15, 1992, p. 73.

[128] "Destruida escuela en combates," *El Mundo*, November 22, 1991.

forced themselves into the homes of non-combatants, putting them in the direct line of fire.[129]

Guerrillas also recur regularly to murder, kidnapping, torture, extortion, and the mining of civilian areas. Of the 1,144 kidnappings police recorded in 1992, a little over half, or 632, were attributed to guerrillas.[130] Although the total number of kidnappings, both by guerrillas, common criminals, and others, dropped by thirty-five percent in 1993 according to police, the tactic remains an important one for guerrillas.[131]

Especially reprehensible is the kidnapping of local authorities and journalists, to threaten them into abandoning positions critical of guerrillas. In April 1993 guerrillas kidnapped *El Espacio* editor Jaime Ardila, releasing him after more than a month in captivity. Far from denying it, guerrillas have told the press that kidnapping "is a way to make money to survive."[132]

Finally, attacks on oil pipelines have not only caused loss of life but serious environmental damage. From January to mid-June, 1992, for example, the ELN attacked the Caño Limón-Coveñas pipeline twenty-four times, causing the loss of 80,000 barrels of crude. Oil workers sent to repair the pipeline have been attacked. Two technicians were badly wounded on June 13, 1992, when they stepped on a *"quiebrapatas"* (foot-breaker) mine left by the ELN to impede repair.[133]

---

[129] Justicia y Paz, *"Informe de los hechos sucedidos en los corregimientos de Tiquisio y Puerto Coca (Municipios de Pinillos, Departamento de Bolívar), 1988-1990,"* September, 1990, p. 2.

[130] "Medellín, la más violenta," *El Mundo*, March 23, 1993.

[131] "34.5 percent ha disminuido el secuestro en 1993: Dijin," *El Tiempo*, June 9, 1993.

[132] Ardila's kidnapping ended in tragedy for Gregorio Nieves, an Arsario Indian killed by UNASE during the rescue search. James Brooke, "Guerrillas are Imperiling Colombia's Oil Bonanza," *New York Times*, November 10, 1992.

[133] "A mejorar los sistemas de defensa," *El Espectador*, June 14, 1992.

Environmental damage was immense. A July 13, 1992, bombing by guerrillas near Remedios, Antioquia, caused one of the largest single spills ever, an estimated 45,000 barrels of crude. The oil flowed into three tributaries of the Magdalena River, contaminating it as well as the water supply for hundreds of families and their main livelihood, fishing.[134] This constitutes catastrophic damage to the environment, hence a violation of the ban on causing harm to crops, agricultural areas, drinking water installations, and irrigation works that are indispensable to the survival of the civilian population. Although guerrilla bombings of oil pipelines reportedly dropped significantly in the first six months of 1993 — from twenty-four in the first six months of 1992 to three — ecological damage was severe in areas where crude spilled into wetlands and rivers.[135]

We addressed some of these concerns to the CGSB in a June letter that called on guerrillas "to cease the abuses that are a flagrant violation of the norms of humanitarian law applicable to internal conflicts." Specifically, Americas Watch protested a series of kidnappings of oil engineers in Sucre, Bolívar, and Santander, as well as the wounding of three oil workers in an attack on a Cicuco, Bolívar, camp in May 1993.[136]

Disagreements between the government and guerrillas over conditions for a resumption of peace talks led the CGSB to initiate several national offensives, most recently in September 1993, bombing bridges, halting transportation, and stepping up attacks and ambushes against the police and army.[137] Among the most prominent victims of the so-called "Black September" offensive was former Conservative senator Faisal Mustafá, shot

---

[134] "Alerta ecológica por atentado guerrillero," *La República*, July 17, 1992.

[135] "Colombia Uses Military Muscle to Shield Cusiana-Cupiagua Fields," Knight-Ridder Financial News, July 2, 1993.

[136] Letter to CGSB from Americas Watch, June 16, 1993.

[137] After the government announced a state of "internal commotion" in the wake of the killing by the FARC of twenty-six policement near Orito, Putumayo, on November 7, 1992, guerrillas unleashed a wave bombings against civilian targets, including hotels, public buildings, and banks in at least six cities. In Bogotá at least thirty people died and over seventy were injured in less than forty-eight hours. "Crece ofensiva guerrillera," *El Espectador*, October 21, 1992.

by the ELN at a political rally in Sucre, Santander, on September 12. Through imprisoned spokesman Francisco Galán, held in a Bogotá jail, the ELN vowed to continue threatening and attacking politicians opposed to renewed peace talks. In November, the CGSB issued a verbal threat that members of Congress who voted in favor of passage of a new public order law would suffer the consequences. Congress's Vice-President Dario Londoño was subsequently murdered on November 5, presumably by the ELN. These attacks on civilian non-combatants constitute egregious violations of the laws of war.

As we have held consistently in the past, we continue to believe that peace talks conducted in good faith must be encouraged. No other course will lead to an end to political violence. Tragically, this lesson may only be learned after more devastation and the irreparable loss of life and livelihood for Colombia's citizens. Therefore, we renew our call to both the government and guerrillas to resume peace negotiations, this time with a will on both sides to reach a final agreement.

When this report was being edited, a dissident faction of the ELN calling itself the Socialist Renovation Current (CRS) was holding talks with the government despite the high level of distrust caused by the unexplained killing of two CRS members in in September. Negotiators Enrique Buendía and Ricardo González were killed by the Voltígeros Battalion in what soldiers claimed was a legitimate clash in Blanquicet, Turbó (Antioquia). However, the CRS claimed they were gathering forty CRS members who hoped to take advantage of an amnesty, and were detained and then shot after waving a white flag.[138] Nevertheless, talks continued in October as the CRS agreed to concentrate its approximately 500 followers in the village of Flor del Monte, Sucre, where negotiations were being mediated by Monsignor Nel Beltran, the bishop of Sincelejo.[139]

---

[138] "Cortocircuito," *Semana*, October 5, p. 47; Grupo de Trabjo Internacional, *Actualidad Colombiana*, No. 139, September 14-28, pp. 3-4; and Bogotá Televisión Cadena 1, September 24, 1993, FBIS, September 27, 1993, p. 36.

[139] "Government, CRS guerrillas Agree to Resume Peace Talks," Bogotá Emisoras Caracol, October 24, FBIS, October 25, 1993, pp. 45-46; and "Domingo Lain Front becomes another ELN Splinter Group," EFE News, October 20, FBIS, October 26, 1993, pp. 51-52.

According to the CRS, current ELN tactics, including indiscriminate attacks that cost the lives of non-combatants, "condemn them to lose any sympathy or support... We are sure that the solution to this conflict will not be built from bullets but with considered and sincere negotiation that leads to peace between Colombians."[140] According to press reports, some guerrilla-linked "popular militias" in Medellín, Antioquia, also have proposed peace negotiations to the government.[141]

Since we have chosen to focus in the previous pages on violations by the army since 1990, we have also included here documented cases of guerrilla violations since 1990. Other cases dating from 1990 were included in our April 1992 report entitled *Political Murder and Reform in Colombia*. Although guerrillas are loosely allied under the CGSB, we have chosen to separate out responsibility where possible, since we believe that each force ultimately must be held directly accountable for the actions of its militants.

This summary is by no means exhaustive. These violations take place in remote areas where the task of investigating and reporting incidents is difficult if not often impossible. The practice of the Colombian security forces of blaming first the guerrillas for any violence also makes reporting — and verifying reports — especially difficult. To their credit, Colombia's independent human rights organizations are making a serious and expanding effort to document abuses committed by the guerrillas and thus give a full picture of political violence in the country.

The FARC

The FARC has frequently murdered political opponents, civic officials, and people it accuses of being sympathetic to the security forces, informers, or paramilitaries. Often, guerrillas will take responsibility for such acts, to intimidate others. One school teacher from the department of Putumayo described to us their crude rule of law in an interview:

---

[140] "Corriente de Renovación Socialista del ELN critica a la CG," *El Tiempo*, December 22, 1992.

[141] "Milicias populares dicen que quieren dialogar," *El Tiempo*, June 19, 1993.

It began in 1990, when (the FARC) passed the word about what they called crimes. If a person does bad things — steals or kills or gives information to the police or army — first comes the pardon. If the person continues, the next stage is a warning. If he still doesn't reform, it's the punishment, death.[142]

Such was the case for three indigenous men executed by the 21st Front in April 1993 for allegedly taking part in extortion and bus hold-ups, a charge indigenous leaders deny.[143] In a circular, the 21st Front took responsibility for the killings of Yezid Ducuara Villabón, Argelino Ducuara, and Arnold Rodríguez, vowing to continue such actions to "defeat" crime.[144] Summary executions of civilians who take no active part in hostilities are an egregious violation of Article Three of the Geneva Conventions.

Local officials who publicly disagree with the FARC or farmers and merchants who refuse to collaborate by paying the *vacuna* (war tax) also risk death. In November 1992 the FARC executed at least seven people, including a minor, in four separate departments according to the DAS. They included Caucasia police inspector José María Arrieta, a civil official, who was executed on November 9.[145] Those who are nearby when such killings take place also risk violence. When guerrillas from the 37th Front arrived at the farm of Feliciano Yepes in El Cielo, Chalán (Sucre) to collect a *vacuna*, a war tax, his refusal led to his execution and the massacre of seven others, including a sixteen-year-old girl.[146]

---

[142] Interview, San Miguel, June 16, 1992.

[143] Regional Indigenous Council of Tolima, "El 21 Frente de las FARC-EP Admite Asesinato de Yezid Ducuara Villabón," April 12, 1993.

[144] "Entérese la verdad," 21st front of the FARC, undated.

[145] DAS, *Violaciones de los Derechos Humanos por parte de la Subversion en Colombia*, March 18, 1993, p. 10.

[146] CAJ-SC, "Lost Illusions? Human Rights and Humanitarian Law in Colombia in 1992," January 1993, p. 11.

Sometimes, kidnappings result in the death of the victim. Such was the case for Pedro Nolasco and Ramiro Muños Orrego, found dead on December 29, 1992, after being kidnapped five months earlier in Toledo, Norte de Santander. Canadian archeologist Steve Gordon was apparently killed by the FARC's 34th Front in the De Los Katíos National Park in northern Colombia after being kidnapped on February 10, 1992.[147]

Seven days after Héctor Ramiro Morales and Jesús Agapito Alvarez, police bodyguards for the governor of the state of Nariño, were kidnapped by the 32nd Front on November 10, 1992, their bodies were found near the village of Lagarto, Putumayo, showing signs of torture. Both had wounds on their wrists and arms, evidence of having been bound and hung from a tree according to an examination by the Fiscalía. Both bodies had also been burned with acid and no longer had eyes according to the DAS.[148]

The FARC has also been linked to attacks on medical personnel, a flagrant violation of the laws of war. On October 21, 1992, two FARC detachments — the "Héroes of Cusiana" and members of the 38th Front — intercepted an ambulance carrying the corpse of a DAS officer killed the day before in Aguazul, Casanare. After drenching the ambulance in gasoline, they set it on fire. The body, also soaked, was left in the road for twenty-four hours under threat of death for anyone who attempted to remove it.[149]

The FARC has also carried out bombings of civilian targets causing civilian casualties. In March 1992 the FARC took responsibility for a bomb detonated in front of the Diners Club of Colombia and a Citibank branch in Bogotá, killing security guard Segundo Pino Guisa and injuring ten passers-by.[150]

---

[147] "Urabá: muere un científico canadiense," *El Tiempo*, May 14, 1992.

[148] "Yo también acuso," *Semana*, December 15, 1992, p. 73.

[149] Ibid.

[150] "FARC claims responsibility for attacks," Bogotá Emisoras Caracol, March 28, 1992, FBIS, March 30, 1992, p. 33; and "Un muerto al estallar dos bombas en Bogotá," *Nuevo Siglo*, March 28, 1992.

The ELN

Like the FARC, the ELN frequently murders political opponents, civic officials, and people it accuses of being sympathetic to the security forces, informers, or paramilitaries. In one especially reprehensible act, the ELN murdered journalist and newspaper editor Eustorgio Colmenares of the Cúcuta-based *La Opinión* on March 12, 1993, as he stood on the terrace of his home with his wife. In a release sent to a television station, guerrillas said Colmenares was murdered for disagreeing with them.[151] According to the newsweekly *Semana*, Colmenares was the hundredth journalist killed in four years of political violence and the first murdered by guerrillas.[152]

The ELN also kidnap police officers, torture, then kill them. In one case, three DAS officers investigating a cattle theft in La Guajira were reportedly detained by members of the "José Manuel Martínez" Front of the ELN on May 20, 1992. Two days later, the cattle owners, kidnapped at the same time, were released. Despite negotiations, a peace march by local residents, a direct appeal to the CGSB negotiators then in talks with the government in Mexico and assurances by their ELN captors that the men would be released, the three were apparently executed and their bodies dumped on a nearby ranch. The pathology report quoted in the press determined that all three men had suffered torture. They had been burned, their abdomens cut open, and their fingernails pulled out. All had been shot in the head.[153]

Another case involved officers Alvaro Cañas Bermúdez, Gonzalo Espitia Otálora, and José Riviero Gómez Rojas, kidnapped by the ELN near Tona, Santander, in November. Despite a similar attempt to negotiate their release, their bodies were found on November 15 showing signs of torture,

---

[151] "ELN se atribuye crimen de director de La Opinión," *La Prensa*, March 17, 1993; and Letter to Americas Watch from the Committee to Protect Journalists, August 11, 1993.

[152] "Nueva pesadilla," *Semana*, March 23, 1993, pp. 30-31.

[153] "Yo también acuso," *Semana*, December 15, 1992, p. 74; and *Miami Herald*, June 29, 1992.

including cuts and burns. A report by the forensic pathologist who examined the bodies was quoted in the press as concluding that the men had been tortured with needles, nail clippers, and knives, and the wrists of one captive were dislocated and fractured. Riviero had apparently been whipped with chains and barbed wire. His testicles were also punctured and he had been shot in the head.[154]

Three military officers flying with ten other passengers and the three-member crew of an Aerotaca flight between Yopal, Casanare, and Arauca were executed by the ELN soon after being kidnapped on May 16, 1992. According to the Defense Ministry, they were unarmed at the time and their bodies showed signs of torture.[155] The crew members were kept twenty-eight days under constant threat of death before being released.[156]

Other state employees have also been killed while in the custody of the ELN. For instance, engineer Oscar Tamayo Romero, employed by the state-run oil company (ECOPETROL), was apparently kidnapped by the ELN on March 27. When his body was found a week later, medical examiners concluded that he must have been killed with two shots to the head soon after he was kidnapped.

Four other engineers remain kidnapped by the ELN, which has acknowledged responsibility for the kidnapping. With this act, they claimed to "[express] our rejection of the policy of repeatedly giving away our petroleum reserves." During the last of the four kidnappings, of engineer Jorge Silgado, three ECOPETROL workers were seriously wounded.[157]

In addition the ELN murders those it accuses of opposing them or providing information to the security forces. In September, for instance,

---

[154] "Yo también acuso," *Semana*, December 15, 1992, p. 72.

[155] "Comunicado de Mindefensa," *Nuevo Siglo*, May 19, 1992.

[156] "Liberados tripulantes del avión Aerotaca," *El Espectador*, June 13, 1992.

[157] Letter to Americas Watch from César Santiago, Treasurer, ACIPET, May 28; ECOPETROL press release, May 26; Unión Sindical Obrera press release, May 25; "ECOPETROL: asesinado jefe de producción," *El Tiempo*, April 3; and Letter to CGSB from Americas Watch, June 16, 1993.

the ELN is believed to have killed brothers Miguel and Francisco Alvear in the Middle Magdalena, accusing them of working with the army.[158]

The ELN also makes a practice of threatening local authorities with death for failing to comply with their edicts or kidnapping them for indoctrination sessions or a threatened "revolutionary trial" for alleged corruption. In one of the largest single kidnappings of this type, the ELN seized twelve local authorities from Pailitas, Cesar, in November 1991. All were later released unharmed.[159] Five months later, four mayors in the department of Cesar reportedly resigned after receiving death threats from the ELN. On April 5, 1992, Alfonso Niz Saavedra, the mayor of Simití, Bolívar, and his wife, Gilma Delgado, were kidnapped by the "José Solano Sepúlveda" column of the ELN.

Along with this couple, the ELN had kidnapped two railroad employees and a representative of the state-sponsored investment program known as the National Rehanbilitation Plan (PNR). The hostages were held for four days before being released.[160] A month later, the ELN kidnapped six mayors in the departments of Norte de Santander, Arauca, and Casanare and kept them for several days before letting them go.[161]

Targets have also included foreigners and diplomatic representatives. For instance, in July 1993, the ELN was reported to have kidnapped Giuseppi Guarigla Naryussy, an honorary consul for Italy.[162] The

---

[158] Revista de CREDHOS, January 1993, p. 8.

[159] "ELN pide investigación de la Procuraduría en Pailitas," *El Tiempo*, November 28, 1991.

[160] "Secuestrado alcalde de Simití, Bolívar," *La Prensa*, April 7, 1992; and "Liberados alcalde y funcionario del PNR," *El Tiempo*, February 3, 1992.

[161] "Four mayors kidnapped in guerrilla attacks," *Miami Herald*, June 4, 1992; and "Liberados alcaldes de Puerto Rondón y la Montañita," *El Espectador*, May 26, 1992.

[162] "Guerrillas kidnap Italian consul," *Miami Herald*, July 9, 1993.

diplomat's body was found on November 18, apparently abandoned after he died of a heart attack.[163]

In combat the ELN has attempted to use the civilian population as a shield against attack. Such was apparently the case during a confrontation between the Counterguerrilla Battalion No. 5 "Los Guanes" and the Efraín Pabón Pabón Front near Santa Bárbara, Santander, on October 7, 1992. Eight civilians and five guerrillas were killed while fourteen civilians and three soldiers were wounded. The Ministry of Defense later reported that guerrillas had taken cover behind the civilians. While the army should be condemned for firing upon civilians, guerrillas share responsibility for forcing them into the line of fire.[164]

The ELN has also been implicated in the bombing of civilian targets in an effort to spread terror. On June 9, 1992, the ELN announced a new offensive against certain media outlets, which it claimed have waged a "disinformation campaign" against them. ELN units then attacked radio stations belonging to the state-owned Caracol network.[165] Both the Association of Colombian Dailies (Andiarios) and the Associations of Media Outlets (Asomedios) rightly termed this a "threat... against the Colombian people and one of the essential rights of democracy."[166] At the year's end, the ELN was linked to the bombings of four Bogotá hotels, injuring ten, including a seven-year-old girl and two high school students being honored for their scholarship.[167]

One of the most frequent violations committed by the ELN is the mining of civilian areas, causing incalculable harm to the local population, especially children. On February 12, 1992, three children playing in a park

---

[163] "Police Recover Body of Kidnapped Diplomat," *Raleigh News and Observer*, November 19, 1993.

[164] CAJ-SC, "Lost Illusions? Human Rights and Humanitarian Law in Colombia in 1992, p. 12.

[165] "Comunicado del ELN," *El Tiempo*, June 10, 1992.

[166] "Medios no cederán su independencia," *El Tiempo*, June 12, 1992.

[167] "10 heridos por bombas del ELN," *El Tiempo*, December 10, 1992.

were killed in San Vicente de Chucurí when the ELN detonated a mine beneath a military convoy passing nearby. Five other children were wounded.[168]

Less than a week later, a woman was killed and her mother and daughter seriously injured when she stepped on a "foot-breaker" mine left by the ELN near El Carmen de Chucurí.[169] During the first six months of 1992, the military estimates that ELN mines caused the deaths of six civilians and injuries to thirteen more.[170]

The EPL

Since negotiating an amnesty with the government in March 1991, the guerrilla group known as the Popular Liberation Army became the Hope, Peace and Liberty party and presented candidates at the local and national level as part of the ADM-19. A contingent of 667 militants accepted the amnesty, turning over their weapons in exchange for guarantees of political freedom and assistance in returning to civilian life.

Ex-combatants, concentrated in the northern Colombian departments of Antioquia, Bolívar, Córdoba, and Santander, were eligible to receive grants and loans from the government to start business projects. In 1991 the Hope, Peace and Liberty party was given two seats in the National Constituent Assembly, then drafting a new constitution.[171]

---

[168] "Perecen 3 niños al estallar bomba del ELN," *El Espectador*, February 13, 1992; and "La Violencia golpea al futuro del país," *El Espectador*, March 1, 1992.

[169] "Otro muerto al estallar mina guerrillera," *El Mundo*, February 20, 1992.

[170] "Desmanetlada una fábrica de minas 'quiebrapatas' del ELN," *La Prensa*, June 16, 1992.

[171] This program was haunted by many of the same problems that crippled a similar plan, instituted after a peace accord with the FARC, that was meant to bring ex-FARC militants into public life. These included inadequate security measures for amnestied guerrillas, who immediately found themselves prey to a wide range of official and unofficial killers. In addition, Hope, Peace and Liberty members charge that promised PNR grants and loans have not materialized.

However, a dissident faction of the EPL rejected the amnesty and chose to continue armed struggle. Led by EPL founder Fernando Caraballo, the EPL continues to carry out murder, kidnapping for ransom, and extortion. Among their main targets are Hope, Peace and Liberty members, known as "*los reinsertados*," considered traitors for accepting the amnesty. According to an October 1992 report by the Public Defender's office on the killings of members of the UP and the Hope, Peace and Liberty movement, the faction led by Caraballo and co-commander Danilo Trujillo "is readying itself to finish off those who were their comrades in the armed struggle and who have today returned to the country's political life."[172]

Information provided to the Public Defender's office by the Hope, Peace and Liberty movement indicated that in the eighteen months since turning in their weapons, at least 113 *reinsertados* have been murdered, most in the banana-growing region of Antioquia known as Urabá. Two *reinsertados* have "disappeared." An additional forty-six people have either survived attacks or been threatened with death directly.[173] Information supplied to the Public Defender subsequently by the "Progress Foundation," associated with Hope, Peace and Liberty, added an additional twenty-six murders, some allegedly carried out by the FARC through its urban militias (*milicias bolivarianas*).[174] This means that one out of every six *reinsertados* has been killed since the amnesty was negotiated.

In May 1993 the EPL kidnapped parish priest Javier Cirujano Arjona San Jacinto, Bolivar. Cirujano, seventy-four, had been involved in the reintegration of the EPL faction demobilised in the San Jacinto area in 1991. After his badly decomposed body was found forty-five days later, the EPL informed a Bogota radio station that he had been subjected to a "popular trial" for his work.

The Hope, Peace and Liberty party believes the majority of murders are the work of the dissident EPL, which apparently intends to force its ex-

---

[172] Defensoría del Pueblo, *Estudio del caso de Homicidio de Miembros de la Unión Patriótica y Esperanza, Paz y Libertad*, pp. 53-54.

[173] *Ibid.*

[174] Fundación Progresar, "*Recientes homicidios cometidos contra miembros de 'Esperanza, Paz y Libertad' y obreros bananeros de Urabá*," March 15, 1993.

colleagues away from the National Union of Agricultural Industry Workers (SINTRAINAGRO), which the guerrillas seek to control. SINTRAINAGRO represents over 13,600 banana workers in Urabá alone, and is one of Colombia's largest and most powerful unions.[175] On February 27, 1993, SINTRAINAGRO secretary general José Oliverio Molina was shot down after heavily-armed men forced him into a vehicle as he was waiting for a taxi outside his Medellín hotel.[176] Four months later, SINTRAINAGRO militant and UP city council member Antonio Benítez was murdered in circircumstances that have yet to be clarified.[177] In addition *los reinsertados* are targetted by paramilitaries, the army, relatives of victims of the EPL, and *sicarios*.[178]

On March 8, about 25,000 workers went on an indefinite strike to protest paramilitary violence in Urabá. Over the previous three weeks, more than forty people had been reported murdered.[179] According to Hope, Peace and Liberty senator Aníbal Palacios, violence is causing new self-defense groups to form. "It's a very worrisome situation because threats, blackmail, and assassination have brought about the formation of new self-defense groups."[180]

---

[175] *Ibid.*, pg. 56.

[176] "Union leader slain outside Medellín hotel," *Miami Herald*, February 28, 1993.

[177] "El Trimestre en sucesos," *Cien Días*, Vol. 6, No. 23, July-September, 1993, p. 31.

[178] Ibid., p. 57; and "Quien mata al EPL?" *El Espectador*, May 10, 1992.

[179] "Banana Workers Strike to Protest Violence," *Miami Herald*, March 9, 1993.

[180] "Nacen más grupos de autodefensa," *La Prensa*, April 21, 1992.

PART III

UNITED STATES POLICY

As this report has documented, the Colombian security forces, including the Mobile Brigades, are responsible for massive and deplorable abuses against the civilian population. At the same time, most of the materiel used by and training provided the Colombian army and police come from the United States.

The bulk of military items donated or sold to Colombia since 1989 have been provided under the guise of the war on drugs. In fact, however, the line between counterinsurgency and counter-narcotics is thinly drawn. This is not only because the dominant view held in the U.S. government is that the guerrillas have "evolved into criminal organizations, heavily involved in narcotics trafficking,"[1] but also because the Colombian armed forces themselves have placed a higher priority in recent years on the anti-guerrilla struggle.

In addition, there are not effective mechanisms to ensure that the weapons transferred for anti-narcotics operations are not diverted for other purposes. According to the U.S. General Accounting Office (GAO) in August 1993, "U.S. military officials had not fully implemented end-use monitoring procedures to ensure that Colombia's military is using aid primarily for counter-narcotics purposes."[2] End-use monitoring is also a human rights issue. The GAO's report said that the State Department had not established procedures to ensure that U.S. assistance did not go to units where individuals had abused human rights. The GAO found "two instances

---

[1] U.S. Department of Defense, *Congressional Presentation for Security Assistance Programs, Fiscal Year 1994*, p. 151. The CPD listed as the first objective of U.S. programs to "support Colombia's efforts to strengthen and sustain democracy, with particular emphasis on counter-insurgency/counter-narcotics efforts." Despite that choice of wording, Pentagon officials stressed to Americas Watch that the focus of U.S. efforts in Colombia remains on counter-narcotics, not counter-guerrilla activities.

[2] U.S. General Accounting Office, *The Drug War: Colombia is Undertaking Antidrug Programs, but Impact is Uncertain*, August 1993, p. 6.

where personnel who had allegedly committed human rights abuses came from units that received U.S. aid."[3]

The quantity of U.S. aid going to Colombia, the lack of end-use controls, and the involvement of Colombian agents in systematic human rights abuses ought to be cause for a scandal. Colombia is now the largest recipient of U.S. military aid in Latin America, and has been for the last four years, with military aid totalling $227 million between fiscal years 1990 and 1993.[4] Since fiscal year 1984, Colombia has had the largest International Military Education and Training (IMET) program in the hemisphere in terms of students trained, and the largest in dollar terms since fiscal year 1989.[5] Between fiscal years 1984 and 1992, 6,844 Colombian soldiers were trained under IMET, more than triple the number from El Salvador, where the United States was heavily involved in a counterinsurgency war; over 2,000 military and police were trained in U.S. schools between fiscal year 1990 and 1992 alone.[6] U.S. officials insist that the United States tracks these students through military-to-military contacts,[7] but it is doubtful that the involvement of U.S.-trained personnel in human rights abuses comes to light in any but the most egregious cases.

Despite efforts by U.S. government officials to emphasize the anti-narcotics component of U.S. assistance, the priority for the Colombian armed forces remains counterinsurgency. The United States acknowledged as much when in early 1992 it re-directed U.S. aid to the police, Air Force, and Navy, and away from the army, a move also related to the

---

[3] Ibid., p. 6.

[4] U.S. Department of Defense, Defense Security Assistance Agency, *Fiscal Year Series As of September 30, 1992*, pp. 364-65. Fiscal Year 1993 data provided by Senate Foreign Relations Committee staff.

[5] U.S. Department of Defense, Defense Security Assistance Agency, *Foreign Military Construction Sales and Military Assistance Facts as of September 30, 1991*, pp. 104-5 and 97.

[6] U.S. Department of Defense, Defense Security Assistance Agency, *Fiscal Year Series*, pp. 365 and 381; GAO, "The Drug War," p. 47.

[7] U.S. Department of Defense, telephone interview, November 24, 1993.

army's ineffectiveness in anti-drug operations.[8] In the early days of the drug war, Colombian military officers were quite explicit about their intent to use anti-narcotics monies for counterinsurgency, telling congressional staff members that the majority of aid provided under the counter-narcotics Andean Initiative would be used to launch a major new offensive against the guerrillas.[9] Such proclivities were given sanction by U.S. officials. According to former U.S. Ambassador to Colombia Thomas MacNamara in mid-1991, "I don't see the utilization of the arms against the guerrillas as a deviation. The arms are given to the government in order that it may use them in the anti-narcotics struggle...but this is not a requirement of the United States."[10]

The Colombian armed forces' preoccupation with the counterinsurgency war has continued. The head of the Colombian Air Force, Major General Alfonso Abondano Alzamora told the Colombian press in February 1993 that the Air Force was mounting an ambitious aerial counterinsurgency program, announcing the purchase of sixteen U.S.-made UH-1H and Blackhawk helicopters, to be used "for the support of ground troops."[11] Abondano also said that steps were underway to

---

[8] Americas Watch, *Political Murder and Reform*, p. 110; Washington Office on Latin America, *The Colombian National Police, Human Rights and U.S. Drug Policy* (Washington, D.C.: Washington Office on Latin America, May 1993), p. 7.

[9] The offensive, known as "Operation Tri-Color 90," began on April 1, 1990, involving one-quarter of Colombia's army and a large portion of the Air Force. U.S. Congress, House, Committee on Government Operations, *Stopping the Flood of Cocaine With Operation Snowcap: Is It Working?*, Thirteenth Report, 101st Congress, 2d Session (Washington, D.C.: U.S. Government Printing Office, 1990), p. 83.

[10] Washington Office on Latin America, *Clear and Present Dangers: The U.S. Military and the War on Drugs in the Andes* (Washington, D.C.: Washington Office on Latin America, October 1991), pp. 52-53, cited in Kate Doyle, "Drug War: A Quietly Escalating Failure," *NACLA Report on the Americas*, Vo. 26, No. 5, May 1993, p. 33.

[11] *El Espectador*, "FAC Adds Helicopters to Counterinsurgency Program," FBIS, March 12, 1993, p. 18.

purchase "real combat helicopters" to serve as gunships.[12] According to the Colombian press, five of the Blackhawks were to "be available to the brigades in the field" before March 1994.[13] This contradicted statements by U.S. officials that assistance to the Air Force was primarily for counter-narcotics purposes.

While the same equipment may be appropriate for anti-drug and anti-guerrilla operations, the lack of end-use controls has been a longstanding problem. Most of the dual-use equipment was, in fact, designed explicitly for counterinsurgency purposes. Documents received by Human Rights Watch under the Freedom of Information Act and information available from the GAO indicate that equipment transferred ostensibly for anti-narcotics purposes includes: 15 OV-10 "Bronco" aircraft; 700 MK-82 bombs; 3,500 2.75-inch warheads; 5,000 40mm grenades; 2,500 M18A1 land mines; 10,000 M-14 rifles; $84 million worth of UH-60 Blackhawk helicopters and spares; C-130 transport aircraft; 8 A-37 "Dragonfly" counterinsurgency jets and another 8 T-37 trainer planes; UH-1H helicopters and spares; tactical intelligence command, control, communications, and intelligence systems; and thousands of machine guns, pistols, shotguns, grenade launchers, revolvers along with corresponding ammunition (see Appendix II).[14]

A September 1991 GAO report indicated that U.S. officials did not "have sufficient oversight to provide assurances that the aid is being used as intended for counternarcotics purposes and is not being used primarily against insurgents or being used to abuse human rights."[15] These findings were substantially reiterated in the GAO's August 1993 report to Congress.

---

[12] Ibid.

[13] *El Tiempo*, "Armed Forces Modernization Plan Outlined," FBIS, November 8, 1993, p. 62.

[14] Documents provided to Human Rights Watch under a 1993 Freedom of Information Act request; GAO, *The Drug War*, pp. 46-53.

[15] Cited in Chuck Call, Washington Office on Latin America, memorandum to Congress, May 21, 1992, p. 1.

The veritable alphabet-soup of U.S. programs that serve as channels for anti-drug assistance also hinders oversight and accountability. In addition to the normal military aid channels (FMF and IMET), Colombia receives military equipment through emergency drawdowns authorized by Sections 506(a) and 614 of the Foreign Assistance Act; Excess Defense Articles consisting of excess equipment in U.S. stocks; the State Department's International Narcotics Control programs (INM), which has primarily focused on the police and the Department of Administrative Security (DAS); Export-Import Bank loan guarantees, normally used to back only commercial transactions but available for anti-narcotics purposes under the 1988 Anti-Drug Abuse Act; the Drug Enforcement Administration (DEA); and the Central Intelligence Agency (cia).

Competing jurisdictions within the U.S. Congress (the Foreign Affairs and Foreign Relations committees, and the Committees on Appropriations, Judiciary, Government Operations, and Intelligence) also impede effective oversight of U.S. programs. According to congressional sources, CIA programs in Colombia are extensive, and have not been the subject of adequate oversight or control.[16] Excluding the DEA and CIA, the United States provided close to $400 million to Colombia in military and police aid between fiscal years 1990 and 1992 alone, ostensibly for counternarcotics purposes.

Colombia's primacy in U.S. military aid programs has continued under the Clinton administration. For fiscal year 1994, the administration requested $32 million in Foreign Military Financing (FMF) and IMET funds, *an increase* of $4 million over the last year of the Bush administration and approximately half of proposed military aid *to all of Latin America*. The amounts were reduced significantly due to deep cuts in the global military aid account imposed by Congress. Colombia is now slated to receive between $7.7 million and $9 million in FMF and $900,000 in IMET. To make up the shortfall, however, the Clinton administration intends to use emergency drawdown authority to bolster the Colombia account. One proposal, for some $60 million, was floated on Capitol Hill in September following a meeting between President Clinton and President Gaviria at the United Nations. The idea was withdrawn due to congressional objections,

---

[16] Interview, December 21, 1992; GAO, "The Drug War," pp. 46-53.

but consultations continued on a lower figure of $30 million in early December.[17]

Despite efforts to maintain funding levels for the Colombian military and police, there are few signs that over the long run the Clinton administration will maintain the "war on drugs" as devised and fought by the Bush administration. The central reason is that a chorus of policymakers and officials have recognized U.S. efforts as a failure: according to the Senate Foreign Operations Subcommittee in 1992, despite the expenditure of over $1 billion in Colombia, Peru, and Bolivia,

> more cocaine was available for sale on America's streets, not less. Few mechanisms were in place to effectively monitor how those funds were spent, and there were persistent reports of corruption among Andean officials involved in counternarcotics.[18]

Louis J. Rodrigues, the GAO'S senior analyst for Systems Development and Production Issues concurred that

> the estimated volume of cocaine entering the country has not appreciably declined since DOD was given its lead-agency mission...interdiction has not made a difference in terms of the higher goals of deterring smugglers and reducing the flow of cocaine.[19]

---

[17] The aid was to go primarily to the Air Force and police for aviation resources. An additional $10 million was slated for Bolivia. Interview, congressional aide, September 30 and December 2, 1993; and Department of Defense official, November 24, 1993.

[18] U.S. Congress, Senate, Committee on Appropriations Subcommittee on Foreign Operations, *Foreign Operations, Export Financing, and Related Programs, Appropriation Bill, 1993*, Report No. 102-419 (Washington, D.C.: U.S. Government Printing Office, 1992), p. 22.

[19] General Accounting Office, "Drug Control: Increased Interdiction and Its Contribution to the War on Drugs," (testimony of Louis J. Rodrigues before the Senate Appropriations Subcommittee on Treasury, Postal Service, and General Government), T-NSIAD-93-4, February 25, 1993, p. 3.

In April 1993, *Newsweek* reported that Joint Chiefs of Staff Chairman Gen. Colin Powell moved to scale back interdiction efforts, apparently frustrated by their lack of effectiveness.[20]

The Clinton administration's director of the Office of National Drug Control Policy, Lee Brown, announced in mid-August 1993 that the administration would "put major emphasis on demand."[21] But the administration's first request for drug control funding differed little from the Bush administration's last. Of the over $13 billion spent for interdiction, demand reduction, and domestic law enforcement, 36 percent was slated for demand reduction, only one percentage point above the last year of the Bush administration. Similarly, funds designated for "international/interdiction" programs declined by only two percent, from 19 to 17 percent.[22]

As policymakers grapple to devise a new anti-drug strategy, U.S. involvement in the drug war continues. In an April 30, 1993, meeting with

---

[20] "A Retreat in the Drug War," *Newsweek*, April 5, 1993, p. 4.

A classified report by the U.S. National Security Council also reportedly concluded that Pentagon interdiction programs had had virtually no impact on the price or availability of cocaine in the United States. Michael Isikoff, "U.S. Considers Shift in Drug War," *Washington Post*, September 16, 1993.

[21] Andean Commission of Jurists (Lima), "Brown's Tour," *Drug Trafficking Update*, No. 41, September 13, 1993, p. 1. Brown toured the Andean region earlier in the summer and said he was "particularly impressed" by the progress achieved in Colombia.

A later statement by Brown that corruption in Colombia impeded progress in the war on drugs drew a prompt rebuttal from Attorney General Gustavo de Greiff, who said that "corruption is rampant in the United States. Otherwise, no one could explain how thousands upon thousands of tons of drugs enter the United States." Inravisión Television Cadena 1, "Prosecutor General Rejects U.S. Corruption Charges," FBIS, October 7, 1993. De Greiff also strenuously criticized the U.S. Embassy's granting of visas to members of the Medellín cartel and their families.

[22] Figures from the White House Office of Management and Budget, in Washington Office on Latin America, "Andean Initiative, Legislative Update," August 1993, p. 9. See also, Ricardo Vargas M., "La Señal de los Silencios," *Cien Días*, Vol. 6, No. 22, April-June 1993, pp. 14-15.

journalists, head of the U.S. Southern Command Gen. George Joulwan said that U.S. intelligence and communications support was involved in the capture of at least nine aides to Pablo Escobar.[23] This confirmed earlier Pentagon statements following Escobar's prison escape that a "small number" of U.S. military personnel were assisting the Colombian police with advice and planning.[24] When Escobar was finally located and killed in early December 1993, it was reportedly because the DEA had provided the Colombian police with sophisticated monitoring devices that allowed them to screen all conversations on cellular telephones. The equipment was programmed to recognize Escobar's voice.[25]

In addition, U.S. advisers have assisted the Colombian armed forces in building military bases around the country. In response to rumors that the United States had military bases in Colombia, U.S. Ambassador Morris Busby clarified that U.S. involvement was limited to "collaboration and advice," adding that "the goal [was] to increase the battlefronts against the guerrillas and narcotrafficking organizations."[26] The Embassy said that four bases had already been constructedand five more were underway.

Given the levels of U.S. assistance to and involvement with Colombia's armed forces, it is inconceivable that evidence of human rights abuses escapes their attention. Yet the Embassy made no public statements about human rights issues in 1993, other than through the State Department's annual *Country Reports on Human Rights Practices*. According to political affairs officer Thomas P. Hamilton, "throughout the year the Ambassador and other representatives of the Embassy pursue our Human Rights Policy

---

[23] "Gringos dirigen el Bloque de Búsqueda," *La Prensa*, May 3, 1993; Newsday, "On the run, cartel's Escobar retreats to bunker," *Miami Herald*, May 2, 1993.

[24] Christopher Marquis, "Pentagon aids hunt for Escobar," *Miami Herald*, July 31, 1992.

[25] James Brooke, "Drug Lord is Buried as Crowd Wails," *New York Times*, December 4, 1993.

[26] "EE.UU. asesora construcción de nueve bases colombianas," *La Prensa*, July 16, 1993.

through private diplomatic channels."[27] Elsewhere in Latin America, however, experience has shown that quiet diplomacy means no diplomacy as long as the armed forces feel assured of an uninterrupted stream of military aid.

The U.S. Congress in 1993 did, by contrast, take note of "continuing human rights abuses on a large scale" by imposing conditions on U.S. aid.[28] Section 520 of the foreign assistance appropriations bill (P.L. 103-87) prohibits the administration from providing economic or military aid to Colombia unless it first notifies two (and in practice, four) congressional committees, which have informal authority to halt the aid.

In adopting the condition, the Senate "urge[d] the Colombian Government to permit access to the International Committee of the Red Cross to police and military detention facilities," access which has been denied on a wide scale.[29] In particular, a system by which Colombian police and military authorities agreed to notify the ICRC when persons were taken prisoner does not function. The Congress's action prompted alarm among Colombian governmental officials, one of whom, Procurador General Carlos Gustavo Arrieta, visited Washington in early December 1993. Shortly before departing, Arrieta had written Colombian Foreign Minister Noemi Sanín de Rubio and other cabinet officials recommending a vigorous campaign to improve Colombia's image abroad.[30] Responding to the problem as one of image rather than substance, however, does little to inspire faith that Colombia's serious human rights situation will be addressed at the source.

---

[27] Thomas P. Hamilton, Counselor for Political Affairs, letter to Americas Watch, September 27, 1993.

[28] U.S. Congress, Senate, Committee on Appropriations Subcommittee on Foreign Operations, *Foreign Operations, Export Financing, and Related Programs Appropriation Bill, 1994*, Report 103-142 (Washington, D.C.: U.S. Government Printing Office, September 14, 1993), p. 32.

[29] Ibid.

[30] "Piden mejorar la imagen del país," *El Tiempo*, October 31, 1993.

Through a six-year, $36 million program, moreover, the U.S. Agency for International Development (AID) has provided support for judicial reform in Colombia. While the bulk of these funds have gone to train judges and provide for equipment and infrastructure, they have also supported the highly-controversial public order courts (see above), with apparently little regard for the potential for abuse within the public order system or the problems of due process and independence of the judiciary connected with it. In a March 1993 interview with Americas Watch, for example, U.S. Embassy political officer Janet Crist defended the extension of the public order jurisdiction to the striking workers from the state telecommunications agency TELECOM, a case that became so controversial within Colombia that it was eventually transferred back to the ordinary justice system.[31] Fortunately, there are indications that AID officials are increasingly concerned about reports of abuse of the public order jurisdiction, and may be willing to press for certain reforms.

---

[31] Interview, March 3, 1993.

APPENDIX I

Bombardments Causing Civilian Casualties

1990-1993*

1990

Jan. 6-7: Farmer Catalino Guerra disappeared after airplanes and helicopter gunships attached to the army and the V Brigade carried out a dawn bombing raid on the villages of La Concepción, La Concha, Bocas del Don Juan and El Bagre, Yondó (Antioquia) and San Lorenzo (Bolívar). One man was killed and six others, including two children, were seriously injured. Houses, schools and a community building along with crops and stock were destroyed. Three days later, approximately 75 area residents remained under house arrest. Three peasants fleeing the bombardment in a canoe were killed by the navy. Although these abuses were reported to the Procuraduría, the paperwork has since been lost.

Feb. 9-12: Airplanes and helicopter gunships from the Nueva Granada Battalion attacked villages near San Vicente de Chucurí (Santander), forcing 1,400 families to flee. Eliseo and Juan Caballero, two elderly deaf-mute brothers, were tortured and killed inside their house in nearby Altogrande during an army bombardment of the area. Soldiers buried them in shallow graves near the house. Farmers Gilberto Peñaloza and Noé Quintero, 15, were tortured and killed in their fields by soldiers and Gilberto Caballero and Isidro Cepeda were "disappeared." Many families fled the area. Carlos Garavito was detained and forced inside a helicopter. His destroyed body was found a week later. Although these abuses were reported to the Procuraduría, the paperwork has since been lost.

June-July: Peasants from the Sierra del Perijá (César) reported that indiscriminate bombings and sweeps by the II Brigade and counterguerrilla units resulted in the torture of five peasants, destroyed crops and stock and the forced displacement of an estimated 2,500 peasants from 13 villages. Virgilio Durán and Prino Pinto were forced to act as army guides. At least

700 families were prevented from fleeing by army roadblocks, which also severely restricted the transport of food and medicines. Indiscriminate bombings in Aguasfrías, Puerto Coca (Bolívar) forced families to evacuate. Fourteen houses were later destroyed by the army. No information is available of the status of any official investigation.

Sept. 4-12: Mobile Brigade 2 bombed and strafed El Bagre, La Concha, No Te Pases and La Poza, Yondó (Santander). All the crops in La Concha were lost and 15 houses destroyed. Families were prevented by soldiers from leaving. A joint government-NGO commission documented property crimes against 20 people, five arbitrary detentions, five cases of torture and one "disappearance."

Sept. 8: Four peasants were killed by Mobile Brigade 2 during an attack on the village of Santa Coa, Pinillos (Bolivar).

Sept. 10: Arnulfo Hernández, president of the La Poza neighbors association, was killed during a combined operation led by Mobile Brigade II in the villages of La Concha, Elo Bagre, Cuatro Bocas, La Poza, Campo de Cimitarra and Caño Blanco, Yondó (Santander).

Dec. 9: With Operation Centaur II, designed to eliminate the General Secretariat of the FARC, Mobile Brigade 1 and other units of the Colombian Armed Forces begin a series of bombardments, aerial strafings and ground searches that leave many villages around La Uribe (Meta) decimated.

1991

May 29: A 73-year-old woman died after suffering severe injuries in the bombing by the army of Cañabraval, Barrancabermeja (Santander).

July-August: Operations by Mobile Brigade 2 in the villages of Las Conchas, Tipaco, Alto del Caballo, Las Frías, Los Azules, Las Cruces and Paladeros, Cáceres (Antioquia) resulted in mass arbitrary detentions and numerous reports of threats and torture. Many detentions were never reported to civil authorities, who later reported the abuses to the Procuraduría for investigation.

July 11: Bombardments and strafings in the village of Nariño by Mobile Brigade 3 killed the son of farmer Hernando Cossio. In addition, the villages of La Julia, Tierradentro and El Diviso, La Uribe (Meta) were also bombed. That day, Julián Buritica Zúñiga was killed in his home near Puerto Asís (Putumayo) and later claimed by the army as a guerrilla victim.

July 19: A bombing by Mobile Brigade 2 over Puerto López, El Bagre (Antioquia) resulted in 61 civilians injured. However, the military claims all were guerrillas.

Oct. 11: Bombardments and aeriel strafings in Coroncoro and Yanacuí, San Pablo (Bolívar) forced some families to flee.

Nov. 1: Helicopter gunships attached to Mobile Brigade 2 strafed villages near Puerto Santander, Vistahermosa (Meta) indiscriminately and soldiers committed a series of abuses against area farmers.

Nov. 19: Bombardments and aerial strafing around Puerto Asís (Putumayo) wounded one peasant. Near Villagarzón, one peasant was killed in a bombardment and later presented by the army as a guerrilla killed in action.

Nov. 20: Bombardments and fierce combat between the army and the FARC near Mulatos, La Resbalosa, Las Nieves and La Hoz, Apartadó (Antioquia) left a three-year-old girl dead, more than 100 people displaced and houses and at least one school destroyed.

Nov. 24: Peasants reported that indiscriminate bombardments and aerial strafing in Lejania, Patio Bonito, El Caguí, San Lorenzo Alto and Yanacué, San Pablo (Bolívar) resulted in the deaths of peasant Alfredo Roldos and the wounding of Tiberio Ramirez as well as the destruction of crops.

1992

January-March: Intense fighting between the army and guerrillas caused 120 people from the Chucurí region to flee to Barrancabermeja (Santander). Reports of abuses by the army remain under investigation.

Jan. 14: Four peasant homes were burned and animals killed during a counterattack by the Nueva Granada Battalion against insurgents near the village of La Legía, Barrancabermeja (Santander). 11 people were forced to flee.

Jan. 17: Army bombardments around El Paraíso, Cofanía and La Castellana, Villagarzón (Putumayo) forced peasant families to flee. They reported considerable damage to their homes and farms.

February 13: Five peasants were killed and a child injured when the XIII Army Brigade bombed near Gutiérrez, Cundinamarca. Several days later, another bombardment destroyed a peasant home, killing three children and their father and leaving one child seriously injured.

Feb. 14: Bombardments by the army near Rio Blanco village left six farmers dead and one wounded.

Feb. 16: During a five-day operation by soldiers in the villages of Patico Alto and Bajo and La Rinconada (Bolívar), peasants report that they were threatened and tortured during ad-hoc interrogations. Pablo Antonio García was detained, shot then dressed in guerrilla clothing and declared a combatant killed in combat.

Feb. 20-23: Durings bombings and aerial strafings by Mobile Brigade 1 in Las Gaviotas, Paraiso, San Carlos, Diviso and Recreo, La Uribe (Meta), peasants report the sacking of houses, arbitrary detentions, the killing of stock and threats against them. The investigation into these reports has since been shelved with no resolution.

Feb. 25: An airplane and five helicopters began an indiscriminate bombing over the villages of Charcodanto, Lindosa and La Hermita, Puerto Rico

(Meta). Soldiers then detained two minors for over five hours, interrogating then with blows and threats for the whereabouts of their father.

Feb. 28: Intense bombardments and aeriel strafings over Paraiso and Santander, La Uribe (Meta) caused some families to flee temporarily.

April 18-19: The villages of Pozo Nutria and El Pueblito, Barrancabermeja and La Rasquiñosa, San Vicente de Chucurí (Santander) were bombed and strafed by the Nueva Granada Battalion. Soldiers reportedly burned one house, tortured one woman and stole valuables and the equivalent of $120 from her home. One man was detained and forced to act as a guide for 18 hours. An investigation continues.

May 11-13: Intense bombardments by Mobile Brigade 1 destroyed two houses and domestic animals in La Esperanza, La Uribe (Meta). In a sweep, 11-year old Martha Cecilia Ayure was killed.

May 12: The military bombed and strafed the villages of Granada, Tambo Redondo, La Colorada, Pamplona, Pamplonita and La Bodega, Barrancabermeja (Santander). Later, 70 Pamplona and Pamplonita villagers peacefully occupied government offices in Barrancabermeja to protest abuses by the military and MAS.

May 20: During an operation by Mobile Brigade 2 around San Lorenzo (Bolívar), a peasant was detained and tortured and María Cecilia Sepúlveda was forced to take off her clothes, then tortured and made to accompany soldiers in a boat for a night.

June 12: Nine farmers, including four children, were "disappeared" during bombardments and a ground sweep by Mobile Brigade 2 from La Conformidad, Morales (Bolívar).

July 14-24: Two days after a Peace Forum sponsored by the town of La Uribe, Mobile Brigade 1 increased bombardments and aerial strafing against 7 villages, causing an estimated 1,200 peasants to flee. Diógenes

Silva, Froilán Cabrera and Saúl Torres were "disappeared" along with two minors. An investigation continues.

July 17-23: Six people were tortured and killed and three reported receiving threats during an operation led by Mobile Brigade 2 in the villages of General Córdova, Tienda Nueva, Peroles, Los Tubos, El Pueblito, Las Margaritas, Las Marías and Nueva Colombia, Barrancabermeja, and El Marfil and Trienta y dos, San Vicente de Chucurí (Santander).

October: Bombardments by Mobile Brigade 1 in La Julia, La Uribe (Meta) were carried out with threats and mistreatment of the civilian population.

November 9: The army launched an operation to punish guerrillas for the deaths of 26 policement near Orito (Putumayo). Helicopters strafed villages near Orito and La Hormiga.

1993

February 28: Combat between the ELN and Mobile Brigade 2 left several houses sacked and destroyed in te villages of La Cabaña, Fortul (Arauca).

April 15: In La Cumbre, El Castillo (Meta), indiscriminate bombings and aeriel strafings left one farmer dead. A month later, continued combat between guerrillas and the army forced 12 families to leave.

* through November

APPENDIX II

Partial Listing of Emergency Military Assistance to Colombia Provided under Section 506 (a) of the Foreign Assistance Act of 1961 between August 1989 and March 1990

Item	*Qty.*	*Value*	*Destination*
Grenades, 40mm, HEDP, M433	5,000	70,000	Colombian Army
Grenades, Fragmentation		299,520	Colombian Army
Grenades, Frag, M67	1,020	12,240	Colombian Army
Grenade Launchers, 40mm, M79	180	129,600	Colombian Army
Grenade Launchers, M79	60	43,200	Colombian Army
Grenade Launcher, 40mm, M79	20	14,400	Colombian Army
M60 Machine Guns, 7.62mm	125	547,875	Colombian Army
M60 Machine Guns, 7.62mm	75	197,025	Colombian Army
Pistols, 9mm, M9	290	62,640	Colombian Army
Pistols, M9	60	12,960	Colombian Army
Shotguns, 12 Gauge	60	6,480	Colombian Army
Claymore Mines	200	17,800	Colombian Army
Claymore Mines, M18A1	2,500	255,000	Colombian Army
Mortars, M19, 60mm	50	31,250	Colombian Army
Ammo, Mortars, 60mm, M49A4	8,000	696,000	Colombian Army
Mortar Round, 60mm, HE	4,000	52,000	Colombian Army
Mortar Round, Illumination	4,000	112,000	Colombian Army
Ammo, 7.62mm	3,000	780,000	Colombian Army
Ammo, 7.62mm		480,010	Colombian Army
Ammo, M882, 9mm		30,000	Colombian Army
A-37 Aircraft	8	833,048	Colombian Air Force
C-130B Aircraft	3	3,564,716	Colombian Air Force
MK82 Bombs	700	296,144	Colombian Air Force
Bomb Components MK81/MK82		165,253	Colombian Air Force
Warheads, 2.75in	3,500	125,335	Colombian Air Force
Launchers, 2.75, LAU-131	24	57,542	Colombian Air Force

Launchers, M260, 2.75 7 Tube	20	46,860	Colombian Air Force
MK 66 Rocket Motors	4,250	969,000	Colombian Air Force
Grenade Launchers, 40mm, M79	5	3,600	Colombian Air Force
Grenades, 40mm, HE	72	1,008	Colombian Air Force
Claymore Mines	100	10,200	Colombian Air Force
Machine Guns, M60, Door MTD	20	110,000	Colombian Air Force
Machine Guns, M134, Mini Gun Sys	6	19,740	Colombian Air Force
Machine Guns, 7.62mm, M60E3	15	56,157	Colombian Air Force
M161A1 Rifles, 5.56mm	60	7,200	Colombian Air Force
Ammo, 7.62mm, Link	1,527	307,020	Colombian Air Force
Ammo, 7.62mm		221,104	Colombian Air Force
Ammo, 50 Cal Link		352,000	Colombian Air Force
M-14 Rifle, 7.62mm	10,000	690,000	Colombian Marines
M-79 Gun Launchers	100	72,000	Colombian Marines
M433 Cartridges, 40mm, HEDP	2,000	28,000	Colombian Marines
Grenades, M433, 40mm	7,992	111,888	Colombian Marines
Grenades Hand Frag Delay	5,000	35,000	Colombian Marines
Grenade Launcher, 40mm, M79	10	72,000	Colombian Marines
M60 Machine Guns, 7.62mm	25	65,675	Colombian Marines
M49A4, 60mm, w/F Cart	3,000	261,000	Colombian Marines
Mortars, 60mm M19 w/Mount	10	6,250	Colombian Marines
M18A1 Mines w/ACC	300	26,400	Colombian Marines
Ammo, 7.62mm		78,000	Colombian Marines
Ammo, 7.62mm, M80		240,000	Colombian Marines
Ammo, 7.62mm Ball		52,000	Colombian Marines
Ammo, .50 Cal Ball		204,000	Colombian Marines
Ammo, 60mm M49A4 HE	10,000	190,000	Colombian Marines
Ammo, 7.62mm, M80 for M-14		130,000	Colombian Marines
Ammo, 7.62mm Ball Link		140,000	Colombian Marines
UH-1H Helicopters	12	7,144,430	Colombian Nat Police
Grenades, M433 CTG, 40mm	5,000	55,000	Colombian Nat Police
M18 Grenade, H Smoke, Green	1,040	13,520	Colombian Nat Police
Grenade Launcher, 40mm, M79	50	36,000	Colombian Nat Police
Grenade Launchers, 40mm, M79	15	10,800	Colombian Nat Police
Armament Subsystem M23	12	28,416	Colombian Nat Police

M60 Machine Gun, 7.62mm	50	169,982	Colombian Nat Police
M60 Machine Gun, 7.62mm	21	115,500	Colombian Nat Police
Pistols, M9, 9mm	100	21,600	Colombian Nat Police
Revolver, Cal 38, 4in, BBL SW	200	37,000	Colombian Nat Police
Revolver, 38 Cal	300	55,500	Colombian Nat Police
Cartridge, Cal 38, M41	20	3,024	Colombian Nat Police
M18A1 Mine Ap w/ACC (Claymore)	500	39,000	Colombian Nat Police
Pistols, M9, 9mm	290	62,640	Colombian DAS
12 Gauge Shotguns	100	10,800	Colombian DAS
M-14 Rifles, 7.62mm	10	690	Colombian DAS
Ammo, 7.62mm		690	Colombian DAS
Ammo, 9mm		20,000	Colombian DAS
M18 Grenades, Smoke, Green	2,080	27,040	Colombian DAS
Body Armor		170,115	ColombianJudiciary

Partial Listing of Additional Aircraft Provided to Colombia, 1988-1992

Item	*Qty*	*Value*	*Destination*
UH-60 Blackhawk Helicopters	3	26,000,000	Colombian Army
UH-60 Blackhawk Helicopters	5	36,000,000	Colombian Army
C-130B Aircraft	2	3,073,268	Colombian Air Force
C-130B Aircraft	1	1,620,146	Colombian Air Force
T-37 Aircraft	8	166,800	Colombian Air Force

* * *

Sources:

♦ ASCODAS; CAJ-SC; CONADHEGS; CREDHOS; Comité Cívico del Meta; ILSA; Justicia y Paz

♦ Congressional notification of the Presidential Determination 89-24, dated August 25, 1989, March 13, 1990, and additional documents provided to Human Rights Watch under the Freedom of Information Act.

♦ Congressional notification provided to Human Rights Watch under the Freedom of Information Act.